Post-Heroic Leadership

Miha Škerlavaj

Post-Heroic Leadership

Context, Process and Outcomes

palgrave
macmillan

Miha Škerlavaj
School of Economics and Business
University of Ljubljana
Ljubljana, Slovenia

BI Norwegian Business School
Oslo, Norway

ISBN 978-3-030-90819-5 ISBN 978-3-030-90820-1 (eBook)
https://doi.org/10.1007/978-3-030-90820-1

Cover illustration: © Melisa Hasan

This Palgrave Macmillan imprint is published by the registered company Springer Nature Switzerland AG
The registered company address is: Gewerbestrasse 11, 6330 Cham, Switzerland

Preface

It all started in a rather unusual way for a scientific monograph. The seed has been planted with an idea from Anja Hlača Ferjančič, a brilliant journalist at the trend-setting Slovenian national radio Val 202. "*Let's do a series of conversations with leaders about their struggles and victories*", she said. It felt like an opportunity to get the research about leadership that works across to a broader audience. It also felt like a challenge to try out something new as a radio co-host. We made a series called *With an Ear for Leadership. Because Good Leaders Listen.* During the same period, I also had an honour of communicating leadership research to the popular audience via series of op-eds in the leading *Slovenian Journal Delo.* Ever since, the radio broadcasts, podcasts, and op-eds have been truly well received. Why is it that so many people are interested in research and stories about leadership?

Our societies, organizations, leaders, and employees are in need to learn about healthier and more productive ways of leading. Heroic, macho, and ego-centred leadership should be on its way out. We need more narrative about leadership as a shared and servant process and less about ego-charged leaders as some sort of heroic figures. We most certainly need even more research about such types of leadership. This led me to consider writing a scientific monograph with an aim to provide a more overarching, evidence-based model of post-heroic leadership. A leadership that is both shared and servant. A leadership that is apt to deal with wicked problems of the present and future.

I would like to thank Anja and her team for her initiative and collaboration, and all our guest speakers for their invaluable inputs and kind sharing. My sincere gratitude goes to colleagues from School of Economics and Business at University of Ljubljana and BI Norwegian Business School from and with whom I have learnt about leadership, people, organizations, and life in general. I would particularly like to thank my colleagues at the School of Economics and Business, University of Ljubljana and BI Norwegian Business School for their friendly feedback and guidance. Special mention goes to Ula Kočevar and Lucija Perne for their help in preparing the manuscript. Above all, I would like to thank my family for being supportive in all the transitions that make for an academic life and a sea of growth opportunities associated to it. Thank you!

Ljubljana, Slovenia/Oslo, Norway
September 2021

Miha Škerlavaj

Contents

Part I Context of Post-Heroic Leadership

1 Time of Paradoxes and Uncertainty 3
1.1 COVID-19 and the Future of "Ego-Free" Leadership 3
1.2 Time of Paradoxes 5
1.3 Future Wicked Problems 6
References 7

2 What Is Post-Heroic Leadership and Why Do We Need It? 9
2.1 What Is Post-Heroic Leadership? 9
2.2 Why Do We Need Post-Heroic Leadership? 13
2.3 What Do We Know About Post-Heroic Leadership? 16
References 99

3 Post-Heroic Leadership in the Context of Humanizing Hybrid Work 103
3.1 The Rise of Hybrid Work 103
3.2 Algorithmic Management vs. Humanizing Hybrid Work 106
References 108

Part II Process of Post-Heroic Leadership

4 Becoming a Post-Heroic Leader: From Expert to Leader 113
4.1 Transitioning from an Expert to a Leader 113
4.2 Choosing the Right People for the Job 114
4.3 Developing Post-Heroic Leadership Competencies 115
4.4 Changing Followers' Implicit Leadership Theories 118
References 120

5 Sustainable Post-Heroic Leadership Practices 123
5.1 Post-Heroic Leadership—The Missing Piece of the Sustainability Puzzle 123
5.2 How to Make Organizational Life Sustainable for Followers? 124
5.3 How to Make Post-Heroic Leadership Sustainable for Leaders? 127
References 129

6 Leading Change by Engaging and Involving 133
6.1 Myths and Science of Leading Change 133
6.2 How do Post-Heroic Leaders Approach Change? 136
References 141

7 Building Communities and Collaborative Cultures 145
7.1 Post-Heroic Leaders as Community Builders 145
7.2 Post-Heroic Leaders as Anchors of Collaborative Culture 149
References 152

Part III Post-Heroic Leadership Outcomes

8 Post-Heroic Leadership of Creativity and Innovation: From Idea to Excel 157
8.1 Post-Heroic Leadership and Innovative Working Methods 158
8.2 Post-Heroic Leadership and Innovative Organizational Cultures 162
References 169

9 Post-Heroic Leadership, Resilience, and Well-Being 173
9.1 Resilience and Post-Heroic Leadership 174
9.2 Post-Heroic Leadership and Well-Being in the Age of Disruption 178
References 182

10 Post-Heroic Leadership: Epilogue and Agenda for Future Research and Action 185
10.1 Conceptual Model of Post-Heroic Leadership 186
10.2 Agenda for Future Research 188
10.3 Agenda for Future Action 189
References 189

Index 191

About the Author

Miha Škerlavaj, Ph.D. is a Vice-dean for research and a Professor of Management at University of Ljubljana School of Economics and Business and an Adjunct Professor of Leadership and Organizational Behaviour at BI Norwegian Business School. He is an active as a member of the Scientific council to Slovenian Research Agency. He is a valued member of the scientific community and an awarded researcher who published in prestigious international research journals including *Academy of Management Journal*, *Harvard Business Review*, *Journal of Organizational Behavior*, *Leadership Quarterly* and *Human Resource Management*. He is involved in several international research collaborations with colleagues from top global business schools. He received the prestigious Zois certificate of recognition by the Republic of Slovenia in 2020 for his research in the field knowledge and innovation management.

He published and edited *Capitalizing on creativity: Fostering the Implementation of Creative Ideas* at Work and the Outfit7 case study at INSEAD. His research received attention in global media such as *The New York Times*. Škerlavaj is also an Active Research Disseminator as a radio co-host, podcast creator, op-ed writer, and blogger. He gained extensive practical experience through workshops, trainings, and consulting assignments for clients in Scandinavia, Central and Eastern Europe, and China. He teaches Ph.D., EMBA, executive, and Master of Science programmes in Europe and Asia and regularly facilitates workshops with practitioners on cross-cultural management, organizational development and change, leadership development, human resource management, creativity, and innovation management-related topics.

List of Tables

Table 2.1 An overview of post-heroic leadership interviewees and corresponding chapters 14
Table 2.2 Post-heroic leadership literature review 17

PART I

Context of Post-Heroic Leadership

This book sets out to categorize the context, process, and outcomes of post-heroic leadership. Complexities of modern business environment, including dealing with COVID-19 across its dimensions, along with fundamental functioning of human psychology, require us to make a paradigm shift in the way effective leadership is perceived and executed. Task complexity by definition requires interdependent expertise while its outcomes are uncertain. Movement from a predominant leader and ego-centred leadership towards modern forms of leadership, which put the task and the collective into the forefront, is warranted.

The book addresses these needs in leadership and provides a deeper understanding of context, process, and outcomes of post-heroic leadership across industries and disciplines. Each of the topics is accompanied by qualitative data from conversations with leaders in various fields. These include health care, gaming, information technologies, instrumentation technologies, entertainment, gastronomy, road-side assistance, and manufacturing. Using examples from various contexts help us strengthen the generalizability of the suggested model of post-heroic leadership.

The book provides: (1) conceptual guidance for leaders and followers to understand context, process, and outcomes of post-heroic leadership; (2) evidence-based approach to modern leadership geared towards dealing with wicked problems of the future; and (3) a set of interesting conversations with post-heroic leaders operating in a variety of different contexts; and (4) a platform for further research on the topic of post-heroic leadership.

Contents are organized in three major parts: (1) context, (2) process, and (3) outcomes of post-heroic leadership. The first part will elaborate on the zeitgeist and need for post-heroic leadership. It will also define constituent elements of post-heroic leadership (servant and shared leadership) under the umbrella of the newer-genre leadership theories against the mainstream "heroic" leadership perspectives. The second part will highlight the elements of post-heroic leadership in action, such as change leadership, developing culture of trust with feedback, and sustainable and responsible leadership. The third part will focus on outcomes of postheroic leadership, including resilience and innovation. Each of the chapters will be a combination of a specific topic combined with qualitative data from interviews about post-heroic leadership.

My humble yet sincere hope is that this book will benefit all of us in constant pursuit of healthier organizations—leaders and followers alike, business school students, either at the executive level or master level as well as scholars of leadership and organizational behaviour.

CHAPTER 1

Time of Paradoxes and Uncertainty

Abstract The COVID-19 pandemic has introduced completely new dimensions into an already uncertain world and has revealed important shortcomings in current forms of leadership. We are currently living in the time of paradoxes; caught between the local and the global, the common and the individual. These paradoxes cause increased volatility, uncertainty, complexity, and ambiguity, and signal the need for a structural change in how we approach leadership. I argue that it is the post-heroic leaders who will be able to tackle the wicked problems of the future that are here to stay long after the pandemic is forgotten.

Keywords Wicked problems · VUCA world · COVID-19 · Ego-free leadership

1.1 COVID-19 and the Future of "Ego-Free" Leadership

Let us first talk about the "zeitgeist" in which this book has been conceived, conceptualized, and written. At the time, the COVID-19 pandemic has struck the planet. Hopefully, when the book is published, its imminent health implications will be eradicated or at least contained by the series of vaccines invented in record time. It is evident, however,

M. Škerlavaj, *Post-Heroic Leadership*,
https://doi.org/10.1007/978-3-030-90820-1_1

that our learning about leadership needs to be long term. This is not yet another academic writing on the pandemic. It is an attempt to provide a reflected approach on the wider and more long-lasting leadership lessons triggered by the moment.

COVID-19 can be considered (just) as an example of a crisis in a multidimensional space that has been, during its first year, largely treated with unidimensional measures (Škerlavaj, 2020). Its medical aspects were immediate and so seem to be the economic costs. For a long period of time, it has been less evident and therefore largely underspecified what the pandemic brought in terms of organizational, psychological, technological, sociological, and environmental considerations (Škerlavaj, 2020). From the leadership point of view, it became of utmost importance to understand and manage the interdependencies, loops, and complexities among those dimensions—both in short and long term.

The VUCA (volatile-uncertain-complex-ambiguous) world (Bennett & Lemoine, 2014; Mack et al., 2015) has been a buzzword for quite some time prior to the pandemic. Oftentimes called "the new normal" (Harari, 2020; Žižek, 2020), it is characterized by a variety of complex (even "wicked") problems that are by definition (Wood, 1986) those whose outcome of actions is unpredictable, and interdependence is required in solving them. Beyond pandemics, our planet and societies will continue to face wicked problems that will require better forms of organizing and leading.

From the leadership point of view, COVID-19 has revealed inefficiencies or better said fatal implications of the ego-centred forms of leadership. When societies and organizations tackle wicked problems, there is no room for the ego. Instead, we need leaders who know how to actively involve, engage, and connect all relevant stakeholders with knowledge and resources. We need responsible people who know how to put the task and the team of experts in the foreground and stay in the background themselves (Škerlavaj, 2020).

The mistakes of ego-charged, "macho" leadership are unfortunately counted in human lives today. Sergent and Stajkovic (2020) empirically demonstrate that US states led by female governors had significantly less fatalities due to COVID-19 compared to male-led states. Francis Fukuyama comments on the difference between societies that fared well with the wicked problem of COVID-19, observing that it is cohesiveness of societies that separates well-performing from poor-performing one

(Fukuyama, 2020). In line with Fukuyama's reasoning, Erna Solberg, Norwegian prime minister, also downplayed the role of gender and upvoted the maturity of societies that understand that leadership is not about a leader's ego (Henley & Ainge Roy, 2020).

The ideas of post-heroic, healthier, humble, shared, servant, inclusive, and less ego-centred leadership (e.g. Dutton, 1996; Kelan & Wratil, 2018; Rudolph et al., 2020; Schweiger et al., 2020) are by no means just an academic debate anymore. Still, due to their imminent implications, they deserve continued scientific inquiry. Throughout the book, we will particularly argue that mainstream leadership needs to change from ego-centred, heroic leader figures to ego-free, post-heroic leadership process characterized by sharedness and servant leadership behaviours.

1.2 Time of Paradoxes

The era in which we live and work is an era of multiple paradoxes. The first paradox is the paradox between the local and the global. In the best interest of health, we have been closing ourselves inside our state borders, municipalities, and homes. We are reviving the ideas of self-sufficiency in food supply, energy supply, and in infrastructure activities. We are asking ourselves important questions about how to go forward. At the same time, we are all realizing how limited and claustrophobic is the world in which we keep narrowing ourselves in ever-smaller boxes. We are beginning to realize how inextricably linked we are, when production does not get the components, when exporters have nowhere to sell, when the virus could not care less about national borders. Only intensive global cooperation between the world's scientific, business, and institutional community can answer serious questions through persistent and systematic work (e.g. how to produce a vaccine, how to take care of the economy, how to take care of mental health, and not forget about the environment).

The second paradox is the tension between the common and the individual. Society should learn how important it is for what is common and public to work well. And how it hurts us, if health care, education, science, and other public services are undernourished. We have learned that society is not a locomotive that pulls a string of carriages. A much more appropriate metaphor is a carousel, where each of us and all of us together spin only if we cooperate well. At the same time, it is a time when we have learned how important it is that change also happens from the bottom up and it is the responsibility of individuals, organizations, and institutions to be active and contribute to the best of our ability.

There are even more paradoxes of this kind, and they are not uncommon in times of change. However, this does not make it any easier to deal with them. We perceive uncertainty and dissonance in the perception of paradoxes.

The cards are being reshuffled. Dangers arise, opportunities offer themselves. This is the time for people and organizations who are to operate best in this paradoxical world and come out of the crisis as winners. It is therefore not surprising that more and more research emphasis is being directed towards developing uncertainty mindsets (e.g. Furr, 2020; Tan, 2020).

1.3 Future Wicked Problems

Organizational literature (Crowley & Head, 2017; Rittel & Webber, 1973) refers to those multidimensional issues as "wicked problems", a class of ill-formulated social-system problems characterized by ambiguous information, multiple clients and decision-makers with conflicting preferences, and thoroughly confusing ramifications for and within the whole system. While managing the unexpected, challenges relating to "a group of poorly formulated problems of social systems, which are characterized by unclear information, many stakeholders and decision-makers with conflicting preferences, and with significantly confusing consequences for the entire system and within it" arise. Without a doubt we can include the previously mentioned search for drugs and vaccines for COVID-19 among such complex tasks where the effects of actions are not known in advance and where cooperation between experts of very different disciplines is required.

Even long after the COVID-19 pandemic is over, its consequences will not be. By no means should we forget any of the 17 sustainable development goals of the United Nations (2015). The problems of universal health, clean energy and water, preventive actions against climate change, reducing inequality, and decent work are still with us. At the level of business organizations, these goals are also reflected in the goals of sustainable industrialization and the promotion of innovation (Škerlavaj, 2018). In conversations with the most proactive and strategically oriented organizations and based on the results of the first research in these times, we are also noticing that some trends have gained considerable acceleration during the crisis. Digital transformation is on steroids, much more work is done from home (and we can justifiably expect many more hybrid ways of working in the future), new business models emerge from necessity and opportunity, organizational cultures are changing faster than before.

Complex problems will not go away, and we need to learn how to better deal with them. We also need to learn how to better utilize opportunities for innovation that require multi-disciplinary collaboration in interdependent teams. With post-heroic leadership at its core, we need leaders who are capable and knowledgeable in dealing with wicked problems and innovation opportunities. We argue that these are post-heroic leaders and invite the reader into further exploration of the context, nature, as well as consequences of post-heroic leadership.

References

Bennett, N., & Lemoine, J. (2014). What VUCA really means for you. *Harvard Business Review, 92*(1/2).

Crowley, K., & Head, B. W. (2017). The enduring challenge of 'wicked problems': Revisiting Rittel and Webber. *Policy Sciences, 50*(4), 539–547.

Dutton, G. (1996). Leadership in a post-heroic age. *Management Review, 85*(10), 7–8.

Fukuyama, F. (2020). The pandemic and political order. *Foreign Affairs, 99*(4).

Furr, N. (2020, March 27). You're not powerless in the face of uncertainty. *Harvard Business Review*.

Harari, Y. N. (2020). The world after coronavirus. *Financial Times*, p. 20.

Henley, J., & Ainge Roy, E. (2020). Are female leaders more successful at managing the coronavirus crisis? *The Guardian*. https://www.theguardian.com/world/2020/apr/25/why-do-female-leaders-seem-to-be-more-successful-at-managing-the-coronavirus-crisis

Kelan, E. K., & Wratil, P. (2018). Post-heroic leadership, tempered radicalism and senior leaders as change agents for gender equality. *European Management Review, 15*(1), 5–18.

Mack, O., Khare, A., Kramer, A., & Burgartz, T. (Eds.). (2015). *Managing in a VUCA world*. Springer.

Rittel, H. W. J., & Webber, M. M. (1973). Planning problems are wicked. *Polity, 4*(155), 169.

Rudolph, C. W., Murphy, L. D., & Zacher, H. (2020). A systematic review and critique of research on "healthy leadership". *The Leadership Quarterly, 31*(1), 101335.

Schweiger, S., Müller, B., & Güttel, W. H. (2020). Barriers to leadership development: Why is it so difficult to abandon the hero? *Leadership, 16*(4), 411–433.

Sergent, K., & Stajkovic, A. D. (2020). Women's leadership is associated with fewer deaths during the COVID-19 crisis: Quantitative and qualitative analyses of United States governors. *Journal of Applied Psychology, 105*(8), 771–783.

Škerlavaj, M. (2018). Four leadership lessons about capitalizing on high-potential ideas. In A. Sasson (Ed.), *At the forefront, looking ahead: Research-based answers to contemporary uncertainties of management* (pp. 179–196). BI Universitetsforlaget.

Škerlavaj, M. (2020). New normal, new leaders? Time for resilience and post-heroic leadership. In P. Domadenik, M. Koman, & T. Redek (Eds.), *The virus aftermath: A socio-economic twist?* (1st ed., pp. 347–362). Časnik Finance.

Tan, V. (2020). *The uncertainty mindset*. Columbia University Press.

Wood, R. E. (1986). Task complexity: Definition of the construct. *Organizational Behavior and Human Decision Processes, 37*(1), 60–82.

Žižek, S. (2020). PANDEMIC!: COVID-19 shakes the world. Wiley.

CHAPTER 2

What Is Post-Heroic Leadership and Why Do We Need It?

Abstract The concept of post-heroic leadership is defined, following the dimensions of shared and servant leadership. From the post-heroic view, leadership is firstly defined by its sharedness, focus on collective achievement, teamwork, and shared accountability. Secondly, it is seen as a social process, with human interactions at its core. Servant leadership is composed of six key characteristics: empowering and developing people, humility, authenticity, interpersonal acceptance, providing direction, and stewardship. We need post-heroic leadership to find viable solutions for complex tasks, that include both uncertainty and interdependence.

Keywords Post-heroic leadership · Shared leadership · Servant leadership · Abductive research design · Interview data

2.1 What Is Post-Heroic Leadership?

Post-heroic leadership is one of the newer-genre leadership theories (Hannah et al., 2014), and it combines shared and servant leadership. It is a second-order concept with three characteristics that distinguish it from more traditionally individualistic models (Fletcher, 2004).

First, from the perspective of leadership as a practice, its salient characteristic is its sharedness. Post-heroic leadership is seen as a set of shared

M. Škerlavaj, *Post-Heroic Leadership*,
https://doi.org/10.1007/978-3-030-90820-1_2

practices that can and should be enacted by people at all levels (Kouzes & Posner, 2003; Pearce & Sims, 2000; Senge & Kaeufer, 2001). Within that domain, positional leaders have been described as mere tips of icebergs (McIntosh, 1989) or whitecaps in the deep blue sea (Drath, 2001); they are visible and important, but most importantly they are supported by a network in their organization. Positional leaders are sustained by larger forces and the countless acts of enabling, supporting, and facilitating. This collaborative subtext is often mistakenly labelled as "individual" achievement. The sharedness of post-heroic leadership practices also represents a shift from a single-minded focus on individual achievement and meritocracy to an emphasis on collective achievement, social networks, and the importance of teamwork and shared accountability (Conger, 1989; Hosking et al., 1995; Lipnack & Stamps, 2000; Seely Brown & Duguid, 2000; Thompson, 2000; Yukl, 1998). Fletcher (2004) also argues that while tasks and responsibilities differ depending on organizational position, the notion of shared leadership practices suggests that leading and following are two sides of the same set of relational skills that everyone in an organization needs to work in a context of interdependence.

Second, post-heroic leadership is seen as a social process, with emphasis on interactions and interdependence. Leadership is seen as something that occurs in and through relationships and networks of influence and thus puts an emphasis on human interactions. Many images are used to describe these leadership interactions, from the bottom-up images of influence such as power up (Bradford & Cohen, 1998) and leading up (Useem, 2001), to "servant" (Block, 1993; Greenleaf, 1977), "quiet" (Badaracco, 2002), or "connective" (Lipman Blumen, 1996) leadership. The emphasis is also on the egalitarian; more mutual, less hierarchical nature of leader-follower interactions. In contrast to traditional models, which emphasize a positional leader's effect on others, the relational interactions that make up post-heroic leadership are understood as collaborative and fluid. This focus on the egalitarian nature of interactions suggests that the role of leader and follower is itself more fluid and will vary within interactions depending on (Pearce & Conger, 2003) the "law of the situation" (Follett, 1924) with influence flowing in two directions (Aaltio-Marjosola & Takala, 2000; Harrington, 2000).

Fletcher (2004) also suggests that positional leaders and followers must be able to use the full range of skills and move easily from one role to the other even while their positional authority remains constant. Positional leaders should be skilled in both advocating their ideas and in inquiry and must also be open to "being led" by others. Those who have less positional authority must have skills in advocating their ideas, speaking up rather than being silent (Morrison & Milliken, 2000; Perlow, 2003), and assuming responsibility for the whole (Kaeufer et al., 2003). This focus on the fluidity, mutuality, and two-directional nature of leadership interactions suggests a more fluid boundary between self and others as well as a more welcoming, less competitive stance towards others.

The third characteristic of post-heroic leadership is the servant leadership dimension, itself composed of six key characteristics: servant-leaders empower and develop people (Fletcher, 2004); they show humility, are authentic, accept people for who they are, provide direction, and are stewards who work for the good of the whole (van Dierendonck, 2010). Empowering and developing people is a motivational concept focused on enabling people (Conger et al., 2000). Empowerment aims at fostering a proactive, self-confident attitude among followers and gives them a sense of personal power. It shows that one values people and encourages their personal development (Laub, 1999). Empowering leadership behaviour includes aspects like encouraging self-directed decision-making, information sharing, and coaching for innovative performance (Konczak et al., 2000). The servant-leader's belief in the intrinsic value of each individual is the central issue; it is all about recognition, acknowledgement, and the realization of each person's abilities and what the person can still learn (Greenleaf, 1998).

Humility refers to the ability to put one's own accomplishments and talents in a proper perspective (Patterson, 2003). Servant-leaders dare to admit that they can benefit from the expertise of others. They actively seek the contributions of others. Humility shows in the extent to which a leader puts the interest of others first, facilitates their performance, and provides them with essential support. It includes a sense of responsibility (Greenleaf, 1996) for persons in one's charge. Humility is also about modesty; a servant-leader retreats into the background when a task has been successfully accomplished. Authenticity is closely related to expressing the "true self", expressing oneself in ways that are consistent with inner thoughts and feelings (Harter et al., 2002). Authenticity is related to integrity, the adherence to a generally perceived moral code (Russell & Stone, 2002). Authenticity is about being true to oneself, accurately representing—privately and publicly—internal states, intentions, and commitments (Peterson & Seligman, 2004). A servant-leader's authenticity manifests itself in various aspects: doing what is promised, visibility within the organization, honesty (Russell & Stone, 2002), and vulnerability (Luthans et al., 2003). From an organizational perspective, it can be defined as behaving in such a way that professional roles remain secondary to whom the individual is as a person (Halpin & Croft, 1963).

Interpersonal acceptance is the ability to understand and experience the feelings of others and where people are coming from (George, 2000) and the ability to let go of perceived wrongdoings and not carry a grudge into other situations (McCullough et al., 2000). Interpersonal acceptance includes the perspective-taking element of empathy that focuses on being able to cognitively adopt the psychological perspectives of other people and experience feelings of warmth, compassion, and forgiveness in terms of concern for others even when confronted with offences, arguments, and mistakes. For servant-leaders it is important to create an atmosphere of trust where people feel accepted, are free to make mistakes, and know that they will not be rejected (Wilson & Ferch, 2005).

Providing direction ensures that people know what is expected of them, which is beneficial for both employees and the organization (Laub, 1999). A servant-leader's take on providing direction is to make work dynamic and "tailor made" (based on follower abilities, needs, and input). In this sense, providing direction is about providing the right degree of accountability, which has been suggested as a salient dimension of high-quality dyadic interpersonal relations (Ferris et al., 2009). It can also imply creating new ways or new approaches to old problems, with a strong reliance on values and convictions that govern one's actions (Russell & Stone, 2002).

Stewardship is the willingness to take responsibility for the larger institution and to go for service instead of control and self-interest (Block, 1993; Spears, 1995). Leaders should act not only as caretakers but also as role models for others. By setting the right example, leaders can stimulate others to act in the common interest. Stewardship is closely related to social responsibility, loyalty, and teamwork.

These elements listed above are the six key characteristics of servant leadership behaviour. Together, they form an operationalized definition of servant leadership grounded in the different conceptual models as described in the literature. Servant-leaders focus more on concern for their followers by creating conditions that enhance followers' well-being and functioning and thereby facilitate the realization of a shared vision; servant-leaders trust followers to do what is necessary for the organization (Stone et al., 2004).

In order to provide an empirical basis for the post-heroic leadership model, we gathered qualitative data from across the industry landscape and informants occupying diverse roles in their organizations. Table 2.1 provides an overview across interview informants, their organizations, industries in which they operate. Detailed analysis of each will be provided in the rest of the book.

2.2 Why Do We Need Post-Heroic Leadership?

Images of heroic, macho characters of leaders who have answers to all the problems of this world are still predominant and lists of 100 exceptional individuals are not rare (Allison & Goethals, 2013). Galunic (2020) acknowledges the fact that most of us would recognize a star leader by their charisma, emotional intelligence, and public communication prowess. Common wisdom about best leaders is the one that is search of true heroes that can promise us quick fixes to fix problems.

Each time we are disappointed to find that their promises have not borne fruit. In fact, we should not even be surprised that this is the case. The challenges of the modern world, including COVID-19 and the sustainable development goals, are anything but simple. Authoritarian and populistic leadership styles offer simple solutions, but in practice they turn out to be anything but that. The uncertainty we face in societies and organizations today requires smarter approaches to leadership. It also requires a change in the expectations that co-workers have of their leaders or voters have of their elected representatives.

An interesting question is why we still insist on such outdated and counter-productive leadership models. Especially given that we have enough practical experience as well as empirical insights that archaic, authoritarian types of leadership do not lead to viable nor healthy solutions (Bodla et al., 2019; Gu et al., 2018; Kiazad et al., 2010; Li & Sun, 2015); moreover, they usually add to mounting new problems. Furthermore, we also have rich empirical evidence to demonstrate that star performers heavily depend upon their social contexts and support they receive from their teams (Groysberg, 2010).

A large part of the answer to this paradoxical question can be found in a recent publication (Ronay et al., 2019) by a group of Dutch and German researchers. In a series of five extensive studies, the authors are again and again finding that leaders' excessive self-confidence outweighs their competence. When we are choosing leaders, we tend to make the

Table 2.1 An overview of post-heroic leadership interviewees and corresponding chapters

Leader and their role	*Organization*	*Industry*	*Chapters and topics*
Tomaž Lanišek, Development and Smart City Manager	Ex. Knauff Insulation, now City Municipality of Kranj	Public	Chapter 5: Sustainable leadership Chapter 9: Leader resilience
Anka Lipuščеk Miklavič, director	Mlekarna Planika	Food	Chapter 7: Community Chapter 9: Change
Andraž Logar, founder and CEO	3fs	IT	Chapter 7: Community
Mic Melanšek, founder and head of marketing	Hooray Studios	Family entertainment	Chapter 8: Innovation
Grega Milčinski, founder and CEO	Sinergise	Geographic information systems	Chapter 4: From expert to leader
Damjan Osredkar, Associate Professor Dr., Head of the Clinical Department of Child, Adolescent and Developmental Neurology at the Paediatric clinic; University Medical Centre Ljubljana	University Medical Centre Ljubljana	Health care	Chapter 4: From expert to leader Chapter 6: Change
Mateja Panjan, Front End and Innovation Manager	Danfoss	Energy	Chapter 8: Innovation
Aleksandra Peharda, Head of PR	Mikro+Polo	Measurement devices	Chapter 5: Sustainable leadership
Domen Rozman, founder and CEO	Dunking Devils	Entertainment	Chapter 7: Community, Feedback
Lucija Sajevec, director	AMZS	Mobility (roadside assistance)	Chapter 6: Change

same mistake over and over again—we choose the most convincing over the most competent. To exacerbate the problem of overconfidence, it turns out that it is socially transmitted and even contagious (Cheng et al., 2020).

The challenge is all the greater as leaders' persuasiveness is oftentimes in contrast with their actual competence. The so-called Dunning-Kruger effect (Kruger & Dunning, 1999), which received the Ig Nobel Prize for alternative scientific achievements, teaches us that people with very low levels of ability show the highest level of excessive self-confidence. The most ignorant leaders are therefore also the most convinced of their abilities, so they are also the most convincing in the eyes of those who judge whether we can entrust them with such an honourable and responsible task as leadership. The vicious cycle of ignorance and poor leadership is thus completed.

Another question that logically arises from this paradox is how to choose better leaders, or in other words, how to overcome the pattern of omnipotent leaders who systematically overestimate their low abilities but convincingly offer their simple (and wrong) solutions. Behavioural science offers quite a few interesting insights in this area. In the field of organizational behaviour, a new type of leadership, called post-heroic leadership, is making its way both in theory and in empirical research. It is in fact a family of leadership styles that range from shared (Pearce & Conger, 2002) to servant leadership (Barbuto Jr. & Wheeler, 2006).

What these newer-genre leadership styles (Hannah et al., 2014) have in common is the awareness that there are not enough heroes, and that even the most enlightened individuals do not have all the answers to the complex challenges of the modern world. They are also aware of the fact that the best type of leadership is actually the one that puts the community, organization, and team at the forefront. The post-heroic leaders sincerely wonder how they can contribute, what the point of what they are doing is, and how the world will be at least a little better because of their activity. So, modern, post-heroic types of leadership are not about the egos of leaders, but about their co-workers and the task at hand. Post-heroic leaders actively care about realizing the full potential of their co-workers and all other stakeholders.

All of us who are meeting leaders of every age, agents of change, and aspiring entrepreneurs, on a daily basis know that, fortunately, the reality is more encouraging than the image on television screens. Post-heroic leaders are also found in the practice of organizations, and in fact there are not so few of them. They just do not like to be exposed. They are therefore so much better recognized and appreciated by the people around them and have results speak for themselves. This book is an attempt to learn from a set of post-heroic leaders using an abductive research design to develop and substantiate a conceptual scientific model of post-heroic leadership.

2.3 What Do We Know About Post-Heroic Leadership?

Ideas about post-heroic leadership have been in circulation since the early 1990s. Ideas about its constituent elements of shared and servant leadership have been present even longer and both have grown into two separate and extensive fields. As we need to address both servant and shared leadership under the umbrella of post-heroic leadership, my literature search focused on post-heroic leadership and yielded 68 studies thus far that specifically use the term post-heroic leadership.

Table 2.2 provides an overview of those studies, which are almost exclusively qualitative. Fourteen of them are book chapters, ten doctoral dissertations, four newspaper articles, and 38 journal articles. Typically, authors would rely on an established general leadership theory like full-range leadership theory, leader-follower exchange, institutional theory, complexity theory, and many are focused on post-heroic leadership as an empirical phenomenon, while 23 studies are atheoretical. Despite the fact that several theories used are relational in their nature, the predominantly used level of analysis is a single individual. While they cover many empirical fields, ranging from architecture, arts, banking, education, health care, manufacturing, sports, transport, and more, readers will surely agree that the field of post-heroic leadership is in its nascent, explorative phase and therefore deserves our further attention as researchers and scholars of leadership.

Table 2.2 Post-heroic leadership literature review

Year	*Authors*	*Title*	*Journal*	*Abstract*	*Type of publication (coding: Journal article, conference proceedings, book chapter or book)*	*Type of paper*	*Key theories*
1992	Wheeler, Bonnie	THE MASCULINITY OF KING ARTHUR: FROM GILDAS TO THE NUCLEAR AGE	*Quondam et Futurus*	Cultures typically express and enact their views of power and heroism by the ways in which they construct ideals and norms of masculine identity. The most powerful men construct, express, and perform their local culture's ideology of masculinity: masculinity is transacted most completely through heroic leadership. Heroism and gender are absorbed by a culture through its stories: modes of power and gender are inscribed in story, sustained by language. Few heroes dominate their culture as thoroughly as does King Arthur. From the Dark Ages until today, from England to Asia and the Americas—and now especially in the realms of computer games and science fiction—King Arthur is arguably the secular hero of medieval and post-medieval Western civilization. Since this is so, the ways Western culture both stereotypes and problematizes masculinity are usefully illuminated by an analysis of Arthurian heroic modes. To a remarkable degree, and from its very inception, the rich story-stock of King Arthur subverts	Journal article	Qualitative	Post-heroic leadership

(continued)

Table 2.2 (continued)

				the traditional model of warrior masculinity celebrated in the West. One persistent feature of the Arthur-figure confirms his subversive status in relation to warrior masculinity. This mask of command first characterized King Arthur as vir modestus, the moderate man. That figure of King Arthur consequently provides one alternative norm of empowered masculinity for post-heroic culture			
1994	Huey, John Sookdeo, Ricardo	THE NEW POST-HEROIC LEADERSHIP. (cover story)	Fortune	Discusses post-heroic leadership, focusing on how it will challenge the very definition of corporate leadership for the twenty-first century. How virtual leadership was first introduced when global competition wrecked stable markets and whole industries; Business' move to organize itself into virtual corporations; The goal of virtual leadership–to keep everyone focused as old structures crumble; The two fundamental tasks corporate leaders will face; Requirements	Article	Qualitative	X

1994	Roth, Tom	How the post-heroic leader scores	*Management Development Review*	An examination of attitude changes in companies since the mid-1980s through job reductions and redundancies is presented. It is suggested that leaders do not realize that companies are not running as efficiently as they should. Wilson Learning Corp., which has studied group emphasis since 1985, suggests that creating a sense of collaboration (or post-heroic leadership) is a necessity for organizations to survive. The capacities required for people to meet this challenge are listed. It is concluded that managers must shift away from traditional top-down hierarchical structuring	Journal article	Qualitative	X
1996	Dutton, Gail	Leadership in a post-heroic age	*Management Review*	Effective corporate leadership requires executives to share responsibilities, encourage a sense of corporate ownership throughout an organization and implement a tangible vision. True leaders are able to transcend the traditional heroic role to provide mutual influence for all employees. This task can be extraordinarily difficult but beneficial to the overall organization	Newspaper article	Qualitative	X

(continued)

Table 2.2 (continued)

1996	Harrison, Jeffrey S. St. John, Caron H.	Managing and Partnering with External Stakeholders	*The Academy of Management Executive (1993–2005)*	The weakening of the traditional management hierarchy, the hollowing out of corporations, and an increasing management emphasis on boundarylessness have created a new mind set concerning external stakeholders. Increasingly, organizations are moving beyond traditional stakeholder management techniques to partnering tactics that lead to the achievement of common goals. In spite of these trends, there has been very little effort in the management literature to tie stakeholder management and partnering tactics. This article demonstrates how successful partnerships with stakeholders create such valued benefits as increased product success rates, increased manufacturing efficiency, the development of distinctive competencies arising from partnerships with local communities or government agencies, reduced unfavorable litigation, reduced levels of negative publicity, and favorable regulatory policies	Journal article	Qualitative	X

1997	Thite, M. R.	Managerial Skills in Technical Professionals—An Exploration of IT Project Leadership	*The Place of Information Technology in Management and Business Education: TC3 WG3.4 International Conference on the Place of Information Technology in Management and Business Education 8–12th July 1996, Melbourne, Australia*	This paper focuses on the nature, characteristics and styles of technical project leadership. The literature survey highlights and analyses the poor performance of technical professionals in managerial roles and discusses successful technical leadership styles. Transformational leadership model is sought to be tested in an Australian IT project environment along with other critical success factors. The methodology and the instruments used in the research in progress are discussed	Book chapter	Qualitative	Transformative leadership
1998	Sandmann, Lorilee R.	Adult learning and leading–a shared responsibility	Adult Learning	Opinion. Examines how the term 'post-heroic' leadership has impacted on adult learning and leading highlighting how the American Association of Agriculture College Editors (AAACE) is addressing this change in the concept of leadership. Details on a theme by the AAACE; What is scheduled to be discussed at the AAACE annual conference; When and where the conference is scheduled to take place	-		

(continued)

Table 2.2 (continued)

2000	Bloodgood, James M. Morrow, J. L.	Strategic Organizational Change Within An Institutional Framework	*Journal of Managerial Issues*	We delineate the strategic decision-making portion of the organizational change process within an institutional framework in order to examine change strategies selected by organizations. Managers involved in the process of strategic organizational change are guided by institutionalized rationale from within their organizational field when generating the best course of action for their organization. Key elements of structuration theory are used to demonstrate how the mutual influence that exists between an organization and its field affects the strategic change process. This enables us to portray the change process as a transformation of the organization and the field over time. Organizations are not simply reacting to conditions within their field at a moment in time, but rather they are simultaneously influencing the field as they engage in the process of strategic change	Journal article	Qualitative	Institutional theory

2003	Black, Belinda S.	Women who lead at a state education agency: Five lives	North Carolina State University	This is an educational leadership study based on the lives of five women who held the post of director or higher in a State Education Agency. While much has been written about women in school and district administration, less is known of women who fill the top posts in administration at the state level. This study examines five such women leaders' lives and careers in detail. The study is conducted from a feminist point of view, using a life history approach. The women who participated in this study shared stories of their childhood and upbringing; they described their early schooling experiences, and they talked about the significant relationships in their lives. They spoke of obstacles and opportunities, and of pivotal events that shaped them. The research resonates with their voices and focuses on the role of gender, diversity and gender equity in educational leadership. Findings reveal the values, perspectives, goals, and behaviors of a group of women who range in age from 45 to 60. The study explores their early perceptions of gender, race and class, and how each influenced their lives and careers. Each woman provides her input in defining a feminine leadership style.	Doctoral dissertation	Qualitative	Feminist (standpoint) theory

(continued)

Table 2.2 (continued)

				The study concludes with a discussion of *post-heroic leadership*, *feminization of an* organization, and a leadership primer for girls and boys and their parents, based on the findings from the life history research			
2003	Warner, John Thomas	Post-heroic leadership: Mid-level work teams in manufacturing organizations	University of Phoenix	The purpose of this quantitative descriptive research study was to determine the degree to which post-heroic Leadership affects performance among mid-level work teams in large manufacturing organizations. Post-heroic Leadership is the process of leading others to lead themselves. People are motivated to rise to their potential for the benefit of the group and create and encourage a higher level of socially responsible organizational performance. Individuals are encouraged to act with courage, creativity, with freedom from criticism. Post-heroic Leadership is signified through the emergence of eight characteristics: (a) a sense of shared responsibility, (b) continuous personal and team development, (c) a common vision, (d) mutually influencing relationships, (e) putting the interests of the group ahead of the interests of the individual, (f) risk-taking, (g) team collaboration, and (h) enabling others to act. The research hypothesized that teams that exhibited higher levels of Post-heroic Leadership characteristics,	Doctoral dissertation	Qualitative	Post-heroic leadership

				collected from the surveys and from the observation, would also show higher levels of team performance. Nine mid-level work teams participated in the study. The research study consisted of three parts, a leadership survey, a team observation, and the collection of team performance data. The results of the research from these nine teams indicated that four of the characteristics, continuous development, mutual influence relationships, risk-taking and collaboration, were consistently found in the top performing teams			
2005	Dodge, Jennifer Ospina, Sonia M. Foldy, Erica Gabrielle	Integrating Rigor and Relevance in Public Administration Scholarship: The Contribution of Narrative Inquiry	*Public Administration Review*	A traditional view of scholarly quality defines rigor as the application of method and assumes an implicit connection with relevance. But as an applied field, public administration requires explicit attention to both rigor and relevance. Interpretive scholars' notions of rigor demand an explicit inclusion of relevance as an integral aspect of quality. As one form of interpretive research, narrative inquiry illuminates how this can be done. Appreciating this contribution requires a deeper knowledge of the logic of narrative inquiry, an acknowledgement of the diversity of narrative approaches, and attention to the implications for judging its quality. We use our story about community-based leadership research to develop and illustrate this argument	Journal article	Qualitative	X

(continued)

Table 2.2 (continued)

2007	Rippin, A.	Stitching up the leader: Empirically based reflections on leadership and gender	*Journal of Organizational Change Management*	Purpose—This paper seeks to use two empirical episodes to investigate gendered critiques of leadership. Design/methodology/approach—The paper uses an action inquiry approach by reflecting on two pieces of work, one collaborative and one individual, to reflect on ideas about women's ways of leading, and women's leadership of groups. The work includes the making of artefacts which it uses as a stimulus for reflection and as a reflective practice in itself. The artefacts which it uses are quilts, and the feminised nature of quiltmaking is also considered. Findings—The paper begins by reflecting on the ability of a leaderless group of women to achieve a task in a highly successful and timely manner. It uses this experience to explore theories of distributed leadership in work groups, and suggests an alternative proxy for leadership. It then uses the creation of a piece of art about Elvis Presley and the Madonna to consider gendered constructions of leadership, including heroic and post-heroic leadership.	Journal article	Qualitative	Theories of distributed leadership

	Drawing on the work of Fletcher, it considers why feminised post-heroic leadership is so often vaunted and so seldom seen. It posits the tension between self-abnegation and self-promotion and service and individual achievement as an explanation of the slow adoption of this more feminised form of leadership. The paper traces the emergent process of the work itself, and hints at the difficulty of getting the "right answers" from research participants, and reflects on the role of nostalgia as a limiting factor in organisational research. Originality/value—The collaborative method of the piece synchronises with the ideas under investigation, and builds on the critique of post-heroic leadership as an observable phenomenon in organisations. © Emerald Group Publishing Limited	

(continued)

Table 2.2 (continued)

2007	Woosnam, Margaret Dale	Journey to *leadership*: Women administrators in architecture	Clemson *University*	Of the 114 accredited architecture *programs within colleges and universities* across America, only 18 (or 16%) employ females at the highest administrative positions as deans, directors, chairs, or heads. Despite this statistic, nearly 50% of all graduates from architecture programs are female. Little is known about women administrators in architectural education, perhaps because of the fact that there are so few. The central question that guided this research study is as follows: What personal and professional factors characterize 10 women employed as administrators in nationally accredited architecture programs, departments, schools, and colleges in American institutions of higher education? Additionally, this study identified the women's career paths, characteristics they believe aided them in their advancement as well as in their current work, sacrifices they made in order to advance and as a result of their current work, their current work responsibilities, and their future aspirations. Qualitative research methods were employed for this study. Specifically, the collective case study tradition (Creswell, 2003) was utilized in order to obtain thick, rich descriptions of the cases. Ten women administrators of accredited architecture programs, departments, schools, and colleges	Doctoral dissertation	Qualitative	Feminine leadership

	within American institutions of higher education participated in the study. Each woman held the title of dean, director, head, or chair. Interviews, documents, and observations were collected and included in the data analysis. Within-case analyses were conducted for each participant, followed by a cross-case analysis, in which major themes emerged and characterized the 10 women. While feminist leadership theories were used as a lens and guided the current research, themes emerged from the study that point toward a potentially new, emerging theoretical construct. This new, emerging potential construct requires that pioneering female leaders in male-dominated fields be characterized differently than female leaders in other contexts. Five conclusions are presented that relate to the themes that emerged for each secondary research question. The five conclusions were drawn based on the research findings. The conclusions describe the common characteristics of the women and are summarized as follows: (1) Pioneers; (2) Unwavering Ambition in the Face of Obstacles; (3) Employ Post-heroic Leadership Style; (4) Oftentimes Prioritize Career over Family, and (5) Committed to the Architecture Profession. Recommendations for females who aspire to become administrators in architectural educations and for	

(continued)

Table 2.2 (continued)

				current administrators and policy-makers within institutions of higher education are detailed. Suggestions for future research are presented, including further exploring and testing the emerging construct identified in the study findings			
2009	Collinson, D. Collinson, M.	Blended leadership': Employee perspectives on effective leadership in the UK further education sector	*Leadership*	This article explores employee perspectives on effective leadership in UK Further Education (FE). Studies on leadership effectiveness typically seek either to specify the individual qualities of 'heroic' leaders or, increasingly, to highlight the collective nature of 'post-heroic' leadership. While these discourses are frequently seen as dichotomous and competing, our research found that FE employees often value practices that combine elements of both. They tended to prefer subtle and versatile practices that we term 'blended leadership'; an approach that values, for example, both delegation and direction, both proximity and distance and both internal and external engagement. Drawing on other studies which indicate that paradoxical blends of apparently irreconcilable opposites might form the basis for effective leadership, the article considers the implications of this analysis for the study of Higher Education (HE). It concludes by highlighting the potential value of more dialectical approaches to the theory and practice of leadership	Journal article	Qualitative	X

2009	Soila-Wadman, Marja, Köping, Ann-Sofie	Aesthetic Relations in Place of the Lone Hero in Arts Leadership: Examples from Film Making and Orchestral Performance	*International Journal of Arts Management*	The authors argue for a relational perspective on leadership in arts organizations. They call into question the image of leader as lone individualistic hero in control of events, particularly in terms of how arts processes are understood. Given that both film projects and symphony orchestras feature many hard-working, committed people, the authors propose that the entire team, including the leader, be viewed as "hero." They propose that the perspective in which a sole leader is put on a pedestal be replaced by a relational perspective in which leadership is shared within an organization. In this perspective, leaders and those with whom they interact are equally responsible for the actions and relations they construe jointly. Viewing leadership as a shared phenomenon also highlights the importance of aesthetics in all kinds of leadership processes	Journal article	Qualitative	Relational/shared leadership

(continued)

Table 2.2 (continued)

2010	Baird, Barbara	Ambivalent optimism: women's and gender studies in Australian universities	*Feminist Review*	This article describes the place of Women's and Gender Studies programmes in Australian universities as a way of thinking about the place of feminism in the academy. It begins with a story of one such small programme at a time of stress and locates this story in an account of change in Australian universities over the last 20-plus years. The narrative traces a contradictory domain in which women, feminist scholarship and Women's and Gender Studies are enmeshed. The article draws on feminist literature about Australian universities to argue that while neo-liberal university environments are clearly places where masculinist values prevail, the flows of power around individual Women's and Gender Studies programmes cannot be simply predicted. Women's and Gender Studies programmes are thriving in some universities (on a small scale). As well as institutional imperatives Women's and Gender Studies programmes are engaged by specific intellectual challenges and some of these are sketched with reference to the Australian context. Asserting the need for dedicated research and teaching that focuses on gender, the article concludes that Women's and Gender Studies programmes in	Journal article	Qualitative	Feminist theory

				Australian universities are energetic places for this to occur. It proposes an ambivalent optimism to describe its assessment of these programmes and their viability as future places of work for feminist scholars			
2010	Kezar, Adrianna, Lester, Jaime	Breaking the Barriers of Essentialism in Leadership Research: Positionality as a Promising Approach	*Feminist Formations*	This article reviews the promise of using positionality theory for expanding our knowledge of leadership. Based on a critique of leadership studies that have traditionally maintained a simplistic view of social identities (particularly race and gender), the authors suggest that our understanding of leadership remains partial. Using empirical research results by Adrianna Kezar that examined leadership in a higher education context using a positionality theory framework, the authors describe the benefits of using this framework and the challenges faced by the researchers. The article concludes with a discussion of the implications of reconceptualizing leadership research from a positionality perspective	Journal article	Qualitative	Collaborative leadership
2011	Ely, Robin J. Ibarra, Herminia Kolb, Deborah M.	Taking Gender into Account: Theory and Design for Women's Leadership Development Programs	*Academy of Management Learning & Education*	We conceptualize leadership development as identity work and show how subtle forms of gender bias in the culture and in organizations interfere with the identity work of women leaders. Based on this insight, we revisit traditional approaches to standard leadership topics, such as negotiations and leading change,	Journal article	Qualitative	Leadership theory

(continued)

Table 2.2 (continued)

				as well as currently popular developmental tools, such as 360-degree feedback and networking; reinterpret them through the lens of women's experiences in organizations; and revise them to meet the particular challenges women face when transitioning into senior leadership. By framing leadership development as identity work, we reveal the gender dynamics involved in becoming a leader, offer a theoretical rationale for teaching leadership in women-only groups, and suggest design and delivery principles to increase the likelihood that women's leadership programs will help women advance into more senior leadership roles			
2011	Waddell, Steve	Growing the competencies required for success	*Global Action Networks: Creating Our Future Together*	I once listened to a network leader describe her frustration with a year-long initiative to bring another group of organizations into her established network. There had been seven meetings, and she felt there was little progress. As we talked, I brought up the topic of competencies to investigate particular approaches, skills, and tools that she might use. I referred to a model of eight different competencies that I have identified as key to networks' success. The model proved a great diagnostic tool	Book chapter	Qualitative	X

2012	Anonymous	Business Shifts Call for 'Post-Heroic' Leadership	*Wall Street Journal* (Online)	In a recent report titled "Leadership 2030," management consultants Hay Group identified six emerging "megatrends" that, they say, are set to shape the new world order over the next 20 years: globalization 2.0, climate change, demographic shifts, individualization, digital lifestyle and work, and technology convergence. Constantly connected to the Internet via smartphones and tablets, employees are now always "switched on," and the lines between work and personal lives blur. And, as digital tools offer inexpensive, easy and fast communication, cooperation and organization, workplaces are no longer tied to bricks and mortar. By getting to grips with different ways of working, honing new skills and prioritizing collaboration, loyalty and effective communication, leaders can help their organizations' transition. As the practices, behavior and values of the "new" work force become business as usual, the post-heroic leader will come out on top	Newspaper article	Qualitative	X

(continued)

Table 2.2 (continued)

2012	Anonymous	Global Business Shifts Call for 'Post-Heroic' Leadership	*Wall Street Journal* (Online)	To combat the threat of remote working to engagement and culture, leaders *must* learn to lead from afar, using effective virtual and face-to-face communication. *Back to the books–innovations in science call for technical prowess Over the next two decades, the trends toward miniaturization and virtualization will drive the convergence between nano, bio and information technologies and cognitive sciences, or NBIC	Newspaper article	Qualitative	X
2012	Arnulf, J. K. Mathisen, J. E. Hærem, T.	Heroic leadership illusions in football teams: Rationality, decision making and noise-signal ratio in the firing of football managers	*Leadership*	Similar to practices in top management positions worldwide, there has been an increasing tendency in recent decades to fire football managers when the team does not perform to the stakeholders' expectations. Previous research has suggested that improvements after change of manager are a statistical artefact. Based on 12 years of data from the Norwegian Premier League, we conduct a natural experiment showing what would have taken place if the manager had not been fired. In this case, the performance might have improved just as well and even quicker. Building on theories in expertise and decision making, we explore the data and argue that decision makers may be fooled by randomness and learn wrong lessons about team leadership.	Journal article	Quantitative	Norm theory

				Our analyses support a post-heroic view of team leadership as an emergent, output variable. Exaggerated focus on the individual manager may ruin long-term performance. Practical implications are discussed			
2012	Broni, G. Velentzas, J.	Corporate governance, control and individualism as a definition of business success. The idea of a "post-heroic" leadership	*Procedia Economics and Finance*	Corporate governance is a multiple term which means control, leadership, individualism and business management in the area of corporations and economic systems (MacKenzie, 1992). It represents a whole community of stakeholders, employees and customers. In this paper, we will examine the relations inside the corporations, we will also define the term: corporate governance and we will give the synthesis of Board directors and CEO councils around the world. A logical question that arise is, if the leader of a corporation has to cooperate or it makes more sense if he takes all the decisions by himself. Is today's corporate leaders a kind of heroes and in which cases? The idea of control and individualism is not a new idea but under certain factors it means responsibility, business ability and capacity to any change. Organizational change and ability to control or to guide people and corporations is a unique strategic advantage and make the difference to all kinds of leadership. (C) 2012 Published by Elsevier Ltd. Selection and/or peer-review under responsibility of the Organising Committee of ICOAE 2012	Journal article	Qualitative	X

(continued)

Table 2.2 (continued)

2012	Jiménez, Hortencia	DOING LEADERSHIP: New Models of Chicana/Latina Leadership in Austin, Texas	*Mujeres Activas en Letras y Cambio Social (MALCS)*	This article examines Chicana/Latina activist involvement in the Austin Immigrant Rights Coalition (AIRC) and reflections on leadership. I developed "Doing Leadership" as a sociological framework for understanding leadership as a continuous and regular accomplishment achieved through everyday practices. Doing leadership is not ascribed or static, but rather an action, a process that is relational, non-authoritarian, and non-hierarchical. My findings reveal three common modes of doing leadership: leadership that is shared, leadership behind the scenes, and leadership that serves the community. Doing leadership moves away from traditionally patriarchal and hierarchical models for understanding social organizing and leadership, thus capturing diverse Chicana/Latina leadership practices	Journal article	Qualitative	Post-heroic leadership paradigm
2012	Kark, R.	Workplace Intimacy in Leader–Follower Relationships	*The Oxford Handbook of Positive Organiza-tional Scholarship*	Traditional leadership theories and management practices tend to distinguish between the public sphere (e.g., organizations and the workplace) characterized by control, instrumentality, and rationality, and the private sphere (the home), characterized by emotionality, spontaneity, and intimate personal relationships. Recently, new models of relational leadership have emerged. Within this stream, in this chapter,	Book chapter	Qualitative	Leader–follower

				I explore the links between leadership and intimacy in the organizational context. Drawing on the psychological literature, I define the concept of workplace intimacy, present its different components, and examine how it may be enacted in the field of leadership and management. Then I present the processes of exchange (e.g., communal exchange) and identity shifts (e.g., the relational self-concept) that may underlie the development of workplace intimacy. Last, I suggest a wide array of workplace intimacy outcomes at the individual and group level and point to directions for further exploration, empirical research, and re-visioning of the leadership and management field as one that can foster meaningful, pleasurable, and valuable mutual relationships with followers. © 2012 by Oxford University Press, Inc. All rights reserved			
2012	Quirk, Nika Newcomb	Open yet unbroken: We emerge as a circle of women leaders through an artful action inquiry	California Institute of Integral Studies	Amidst the great change and rising complexity of the early twenty-first century, this inquiry's four women co-participants explored the timely question "How might we develop a social space and a process that facilitate an emergent practice of shared leadership?" An Artful Action Inquiry, co-constructed by participants, provided the structure through which to engage in a playful and reflective practice of group learning, selfdiscovery, and collaborative action over a six-month period. Our	Doctoral dissertation	Qualitative	Systems theory

(continued)

Table 2.2 (continued)

	current turbulent and transformative era *calls for us to develop such post-heroic* leadership styles and structures fostering active engagement founded on a mindful, integrated connection between We and I. Conscious systems participation, whole intelligence, and harmonious collaboration are three critical and interdependent elements in developing organizations engaged in sustainable human systems. There is an identified gap between the growing need for those of us shaped by Western societal norms to act interdependently and creatively, and our ability to do so. The women in this circle of inquiry make a contribution addressing this developmental gap by reporting on their own collaborative emergence as a team taking action to establish a non-profit organization in the United States. Participants found that investing time and full creative presence in co-creating social space provided a supportive framework for the vulnerability necessary in emergent, paradigm-shifting work. We practically and beneficially applied art making, movement and storytelling to the work of envisioning, assessing, and strategizing paths of action. We experienced how engaging with collective intention both confronts us and opens doors to deeper relational	

				work practice and growth-inconnection. Our circle emerged as open yet unbroken, where "open" expresses our individual freedom as brilliantly unique and specialized human participants and "unbroken" holds the reality and the opportunity of fully connected integration in the social and planetary system. Therein lies the challenge of practice in such a both/and paradigm. As we intentionally enacted the metaphor of shared leadership in this research, we found that it is insufficient to hold the ideology of the circle while practicing a separative self-concept. A desire or choice to share power is only the beginning of the work required to enact power-with			
2012	Sveningsson, S., Alvehus, J., Alvesson, M.	Managerial leadership: Identities, processes, and interactions	*The Work of Managers: Towards a Practice Theory of Management*	Three perspectives of leadership are discussed: the transformative (i.e. the heroic), the post-heroic, and the mundane. The chapter concludes that if we want to understand managerial leadership as an empirical phenomenon and as a work practice, we need to base our understanding of leadership on ordinary managers' work. In order to understand leadership as a work practice, we need more theories that are grounded in managers' behaviours rather than in the theoretical and ideological underpinnings researchers and other societal actors assign them. A muddling-through manager who is occupied with various administrative, relational, and ill-specified work tasks	Book chapter	Qualitative	Transformative (heroic) leadership

(continued)

Table 2.2 (continued)

				can do excellent work, while the manager who takes the role of the heroic leader may cause serious problems. Management research should avoid the heroic and post-heroic misconceptions of what managers do or should do			
2012	X	WSJE(1/17) Business Shifts Call For 'Post-Heroic' Leadership	Dow Jones Institutional News	X	Newspaper article	Qualitative	X
2013	Brown, Carol Anne	Women on corporate boards and shared leadership: An exploratory study of board process	Fielding Graduate University	This qualitative study explored shared leadership as a post-heroic feminine style of leadership in the context of boards of directors. Comprising 17 Canadian corporate directors, 9 of which were women, in narrative interviews, directors shared their stories of board engagement in conflict situations. All directors had experience on boards with 3 or more women. The data were analyzed using coding techniques and thematic analysis. Scharmer's model of learning conversations informed aspects of the data analysis in the process of theming. Themes from the data that were consistently recounted as key contributors to effective board engagement, dialogue, and decisions include (a) directors showed consciousness of the value of shared leadership to corporate board effectiveness, despite the hierarchical	Doctoral dissertation	Qualitative	Shared leadership

				environment they work in, including the governance model that defers to the "heroic" CEO; (b) effective directors are independent thinkers and have courage to raise the dissenting voice; (c) diversity, in various dimensions, is valued, particularly knowledge and experience based diversity; (d) board chairs are more effective in supporting learning conversations when they are facilitative rather than directive; (e) relational skills are valued in the boardroom to encourage movement from debate to dialogue; and (f) some gender differences in skills or behaviours, were noted. Key Words: shared leadership, post-heroic leadership, gender, women on corporate boards, board process, feminine leadership			
2013	Fitzsimons, Declan	A psychodynamic perspective on the implementation of shared leaderships	Cranfield University (United Kingdom)	A key debate within leadership research is whether leadership can be conceptualized as a specialized role occupied by individuals or as a shared influence process amongst all members of a group (Yukl, 2006). Since the mid-1990s some leadership scholars, as a counterpoint to the dominance of the former and using terms such as shared and distributed leadership, have attempted to elaborate new 'post–heroic' leadership models (Badaracco, 2001) of the latter, in which leadership is something that involves all group members. These new forms of leadership are often	Doctoral dissertation	Qualitative	Systems psychodynamic theory

(continued)

Table 2.2 (continued)

	positioned as something that organizations can *implement* as part of an adaptive response to a rapidly changing world. Despite a 50-year tradition of construing leadership as a group level construct, little attention has been paid in these emerging debates to the systems psychodynamic perspective. From this perspective there are grounds for suspecting that attempts to implement shared leadership may compound rather than ameliorate issues related to adaptive challenges (Huffington, James and Armstrong, 2004). This thesis engages with the shared and distributed leadership literatures and examines how a systems psychodynamic perspective can contribute not only to debates within these literatures but to the wider controversies in the leadership literature. This thesis reports on the findings of a single, 18-month, longitudinal case study of a senior team whose managing director attempted to implement shared leadership. Using a clinical fieldwork methodology (Schein, 1987) in the systems psychodynamic tradition (Miller, 1993b; Miller and Rice, 1967), this study advances a number of contributions to theory. These include: findings that challenge existing approaches to conceptualizing leadership–shared or otherwise;	

				the elucidation of complex unconscious team processes that are mobilized as a senior team undertakes adaptive work; and thirdly, a more sophisticated and theoretically robust conceptualization of leadership as a group level phenomenon			
2014	Drysdale, L. Bennett, J. Murakami, E. T. Johansson, O. Gurr, D.	Heroic leadership in Australia, Sweden, and the united states	*International Journal of Educational Management*	Purpose: The purpose of this paper is to draw from data collected as part of the International Successful School Principalship Project (ISSPP) and present cases of democratic and heroic leadership from three countries, discussing to what extent successful school principals in each of their research sites (Melbourne, Australia; Umeå, Sweden; Arizona and Texas in the USA) carry old and new perspectives of heroism in their leadership. In particular the paper explores two questions: first, how do school principals describe aspects of heroic and post-heroic leadership in their practices? and second, how do these heroic and post-heroic leadership practices meet contemporary demands such as accountability standards and build inclusive and collaborative school communities in challenging contexts? Design/methodology/approach: Multiple-perspective case studies involving semi-structured individual and group interviews with principals, teachers, students, parents and school board members were used to understand the contribution of	Journal article	Qualitative	Heroic leadership

(continued)

Table 2.2 (continued)

		principals and other leadership to school success. Findings: The definitions of heroic and post-heroic leadership are inadequate in defining successful principal leadership. The Australian, Swedish and American principals showed characteristics of both heroic and post-heroic leadership. They showed heroic qualities such as: inspiring and motivating others; challenging the status quo; showing integrity in conflicting situations; putting duty before self; taking risks to champion a better way; showing courage to stand up to those in authority; advocating for students in struggling neighbourhoods under the scrutiny of both district and public expectations; and, showing uncommon commitment. Yet our principals showed post-heroic leadership such as involving others in decision making and recognising that school success depended on collective effort, and being sensitive to community needs through a deep respect for the local culture. Originality/value: The research shows that we may need to redefine and recast our images of who school principals are today, and what they do to generate academic success for students. Both heroic and post-heroic images of leadership are needed to explain successful school leadership

2014	Parush, Tamar, Koivunen, Niina	Paradoxes, double binds, and the construction of 'creative' managerial selves in art-based leadership development	*Scandinavian Journal of Management*	Highlights: [•] Discourses linking management, art and creativity favor particular managerial selves. [•] These selves are expected to display both heroic and post-heroic leadership styles. [•] These selves are expected to tolerate paradoxes and balance contradictory demands. [•] While these paradoxical demands may be paralyzing, they may also inspire creativity. [ABSTRACT FROM AUTHOR] Copyright of Scandinavian Journal of Management is the property of Pergamon Press—An Imprint of Elsevier Science and its content may not be copied or emailed to multiple sites or posted to a listserv without the copyright holder's express written permission. However, users may print, download, or email articles for individual use. This abstract may be abridged. No warranty is given about the accuracy of the copy. Users should refer to the original published version of the material for the full abstract (Copyright applies to all Abstracts)	Journal article	Qualitative	X

(continued)

Table 2.2 (continued)

2014	Sawer, Marian, Andrew, Merrindahl	Collectivism, consensus and concepts of shared leadership in movements for social change	*Diversity in Leadership*	In the 1970s, 'leadership' was a dirty word for many in the women's movement. Journalists trying to find a 'spokesman' complained of how upset women became if they were labelled as leaders. Leadership was associated with hierarchy and hierarchy was seen as inextricably linked with the patriarchal domination of women. To liberate themselves from patriarchy, women were trying to organise without hierarchy, through collectives and networks. Instead of there being leaders and followers, women would empower themselves through taking responsibility for decisions, which would be reached by consensus. At first there were attempts not only to resist the idea of	Book chapter	Qualitative	Shared leadership
2014	Senn, Laura Anne	Nurse-Physician Co-Leadership: Exploring a Strategy to Enhance Quality and Patient Safety in U.S. Hospitals	Faculty of the Graduate School of the University of Minnesota	Background: The healthcare industry has been mandated by regulatory bodies to improve quality and patient safety in hospitals. The struggle to implement and sustain effective performance improvement processes is linked to leadership, especially at the department level where the rubber hits the road. Although many advances have been made, there is a sustained need to continue looking for additional strategies. A new leadership model in healthcare, nurse and physician co-leadership, may be an effective strategy to use to bridge diffuse power structures found in the knowledge-based, pluralistic organization.	Doctoral dissertation	Qualitative	Plural Leadership

	Effectively used by at least 10% of business worldwide, only a few hospitals across the country have implemented this leadership model. Anecdotal evidence is promising, but empirical evidence is lacking. Study Question and Aims: The research question was, "How do nurse and physician co-leaders' description of their work together reflect their roles and relationships?" The specific aims were to explore: (a) the factors that hindered or enhanced the role development of the partners; and (b) the nature and dynamics of the co-leaders' working relationship. Design: Qualitative inquiry was used to obtain evidence from practice. Eight nurse and physician co-leaders were interviewed individually about their shared role and responsibilities, and their collaborative work together within a co-leadership structure. A deductive content analysis approach was used. Coding started with nine categories, which were derived from an extensive review of the literature on co-leadership in business, education, and healthcare. Cross case analysis revealed 40+ sub-categories. Findings: Nurse-physician co-leadership is a form of plural leadership where two formal leaders together lead a hospital unit, sharing power to build a more	

(continued)

Table 2.2 (continued)

		democratic process, but also taking back power and influence from diffuse sources of power commonly found in the hospital setting. Two essential themes, the Shared Role Space: Moving from I to We and Partnered Leadership: Dynamic Interplay of Complementary Competencies, emerged from the data to describe the experience, and a conceptual framework was proposed. Numerous factors were revealed that enhanced or hindered the co-leaders' role development. The dynamic interplay of co-leaders' work together was portrayed. Conclusion: Co-leadership is different than inter-professional collaboration or teamwork. Clinicians and administrators are offered a toolkit to help ensure successful development of the nurse-physician co-leadership model in hospitals. Researchers are offered a framework to measure outcomes, but are warned about confusing terms, and the presence of intermediate outcomes in research focused on post-heroic leadership models. This plural leadership model is a strategy worth exploring to address the challenges of successfully implementing quality and patient safety innovations in hospitals

2014	Shaw, Sally, Zink, Robyn, Lynch, Pip	Keeping People 'In the Tent': Governance in the New Zealand Outdoor Activity Sector	*Voluntas: International Journal of Voluntary and Nonprofit Organizations*	The purpose of this research was to examine governance in the New Zealand outdoor activity sector. We conducted 35 interviews with key personnel from organisations with responsibility for national co-ordination, education, and membership services. Using Brandsen and Pestoff's (Public Manag Rev 8(4): 493–501, 2006) co-processes framework, we describe and analyse governance of the outdoor sector. In so doing, we provide insight into the challenges facing this complex sector with regard to funding and stakeholder relationships, programme delivery, and personality conflicts. We also contribute by highlighting some of the shortcomings of the co-processes model, and offer constructively critical insights for its development	Journal article	Qualitative	Brandsen and Pestoff's co-processes framework
2014	Sinclair, Amanda	A feminist case for leadership	*Diversity in Leadership*	On 10 October 2012, Australia's then Prime Minister, Julia Gillard, addressed the Australian Parliament in response to a motion put by Opposition Leader Tony Abbott. While the motion concerned the future of disgraced Speaker, Peter Slipper, Gillard's speech was a call to, and invocation of, feminist leadership. Gillard used the occasion to draw attention to a concerted campaign of misogynistic, sexist attacks from the Opposition and some of their associates, not just towards herself but also towards	Book chapter	Qualitative	Traditional leadership

(continued)

Table 2.2 (continued)

				Australian women in general. Julia *Gillard's speech followed earlier concerns* expressed by prominent feminists—for example, Moira Rayner and Anne Summers—about the			
2014	Sutherland, Jeanne Marie	Imagining Dialogue with Other Voices as Part of Indirect, Post-Heroic Leadership Development: Writing Mytho Poetic Narrative as Arts Practice Exploratory Inquiry	Union Institute and University	I designed and explored a fiction writing approach to develop inclusive and empowering leadership norms. As a woman, I experienced myself as an "other" with men in leadership. As an arts practitioner, I used this project to explore the potential for an indirect, symbolic method to contribute to leadership development by writing a novel. I am responding to the problem that other individuals and groups may be excluded from or marginalized in direct leadership and leadership development roles. Thus I designed and crafted an indirect approach through fiction to reform inequitable leadership norms that privilege heroic "Warrior-King" leader types, as I interpret them. By designing a multidimensional, metaphoric approach to leadership development, the intention was to explore ways to transform leadership norms through deeper knowing from narrative images and empathic connection with fictive characters. The ethical purpose of such inquiry is to exercise empowered voice to advance new operating myths for leadership. I found that a collaborative writing process by imagining dialogue with fictive characters offers diverse and unexpected narrative results.	Doctoral dissertation	Qualitative	Post-heroic leadership

	I also found that a post-heroic leadership process does not "look like" leadership based on norms of an individual leader and thus was difficult to portray in fiction without making it an allegorical text. My response to these findings is that the multidirectional process of dialogue and the multidimensional mytho-poetic narrative provide diverse opportunities for learning for arts practitioners—in some cases to move in a direction that contradicted my objectives. Additionally, it was difficult to discern personal imaginative material from transpersonal elements, e.g., I could not objectively critique my own biographical and psychological experiences and perspectives and how they contributed to the fictive character or narrative portrayals. From this I imply that if an arts practitioner wants to imagine dialogue with characters to create a metaphoric venue for empowered participation, then she might benefit from feedback, i.e., collaboration could be extended to include another writer or feedback from readers	

(continued)

Table 2.2 (continued)

2015	Eslen-Ziya, H., Erhart, I.	Toward postheroic leadership: A case study of Gezi's collaborating multiple leaders	*Leadership*	This article explores how the Gezi Park protests in Istanbul, Turkey, exemplify the changing character of contemporary social movements, where teamwork and collaboration are supported and the ability to empower, support, and engage others is emphasized. We argue that the role of leadership in social movements in general and in the Turkish Gezi context specifically goes beyond the creation of traditional leaders. This new form of leadership is driven by the possibilities opened up by other democratic and collaborative social movements and also social networking sites. We look at how a horizontal, postheroic leadership message was conveyed via the posters, t-shirts, and chants used by the protestors during the Gezi Park protests, with analysis supported by interviews conducted with protesters	Journal article	Qualitative	Post-heroic leadership
2015	Samad, Ataus	TOWARDS AN UNDER-STANDING OF THE EFFECT OF LEADERSHIP ON EMPLOYEE WELLBEING AND ORGANI-ZATIONAL OUTCOMES IN AUSTRALIAN UNIVERSITIES	*Journal of Developing Areas*	Leadership is increasingly becoming a major research focus in both the corporate and higher education sector (HES). Previous studies have shown that different leadership styles play a significant role in promoting both employee wellbeing and organizational outcomes. However, at present there is a lack of clear understanding of how leadership style, employee wellbeing and organizational outcomes such as job satisfaction, organizational commitment and turnover intention concurrently interact in the HES context, particularly within Australian	Journal article	Qualitative	Full Range of Leadership Theory (FRLT)

regional university settings. A review of leadership studies literature also suggests that researchers have either focused on the relationship between a specific leadership style and wellbeing; leadership styles and organizational outcomes, or the relationship between wellbeing and organizational outcomes. However, rarely do empirical studies examine all three concurrently. More expansive and pluralist research approaches are needed if we are to better understand the contextual complexities of leadership in the current HES. For a complex organization such as a university, an effective way of examining leadership may be by applying leadership theories that examine a diverse range of leadership styles that may have both positive and negative outcomes. The Full Range of Leadership Theory (FRLT) examines transformational, transactional and laissez-faire leadership styles within a single continuum that may provide a way to concurrently examine how these differing leadership styles may impact on leadership effectiveness in the HES context. In this review paper, drawn from a current PhD study, contexts for leadership practice in HES today will be explored, then leadership studies literature more generally will be reviewed to locate

(continued)

Table 2.2 (continued)

				amenable leadership approaches for this work. Lastly, possibilities for leadership approaches that concurrently address issues of wellbeing and outcomes will be discussed. Specifically, the FRLT will be used as a frame to examine transformational, transactional and laissez-faire leadership approaches within a single continuum as to identify how FRLT may differ from or concur with leadership theories and approaches understood more generally to fit within post-heroic leadership studies standpoints. [ABSTRACT FROM AUTHOR]			
2015	Staśko, Anna Wziątek, Rossakowska, Magdalena Chabińska	VERSATILE LEADERSHIP AS A DETER-MINANT OF EMPLOYEE ENGAGEMENT. DHL EXPRESS (POLAND) SP. Z O.O. EXAMPLE	*LogForum*	Background: The changes which are taking place today, forces companies to ask themselves about the quality of leadership in the organization and whether the existing work in this area supports the success of the company. In the global environment, both social structure and political are changing. Demographic changes irrevocable impact on the market more than ever before. For company it is necessary to introduce new paradigms of leadership to have a chance to succeed in this new environment. The aim of researches was to recognize methods, which allow to improve the quality of management of transprot companies. Methods: Researches were conducted based on literature review and questionnaires sent by employees. Cocnlusions: Leadership agility model seems to be the answer to the question	Journal article	Qualitative	Leadership agility model

	of how to survive in the new world. Concept of leadership agility draws attention to a smooth transition between the different management styles as well as the end of the heroic leadership, (focused on only one leader) and the beginning of the post heroic leadership, where the contribution of the whole team count. In the new environment, a significant part of the company's success will depend on the commitment of its employees, and hence the added value of their work. Model of leadership agility is used in DHL Express daily and build the base for achieving excellent results not only business but also those related to human capital. (English) [ABSTRACT FROM AUTHOR] Einleitung: Die Änderungen, die in der heutigen Zeit vorgehen, zwingen Unternehmen dazu, sich die Frage nach der Qualität der Geschäftsführung zu stellen. Eine andere Frage ist es, ob die bisher unternommenen Aktivitäten in diesem Bereich den Erfolg der Firma unterstützen. In der globalen Umwelt der Unternehmen ändert sich sowohl die soziale als auch politische Struktur. Demographische Änderungen beeinflussen den Markt mehr denn je zuvor. Um in der neuen Umwelt	

(continued)

Table 2.2 (continued)

erfolgreich zu bleiben, müssen die Firmen neue Führungsparadigma einführen. Leadership Agility scheint die richtige Antwort auf die Frage zu sein, wie man in der neuen Welt wirtschaftlich überleben kann. Das Ziel der Arbeit war es, die Methoden, die die Qualität der Verkehrsunternehmen verbessern helfen, zu identifizieren. Methoden: Die Studie wurde auf der Grundlage einer Literaturrecherche und der Auswertung der unter den Empfängern von Verkehrsdiensten durchgeführten Befragungen ausgearbeitet. Fazit: Das Konzept von Leadership Agility macht auf eine reibungslose Umstellung und Anpassung der Manager an verschiedene Führungsstile sowie auf die Abkehr vom heroischen, nur auf den Geschäftsführer fokussierten Führungsverständnis, eher auf die Zuwendung der postheroischen Geschäftsführung (wo nicht nur die Führungskraft sondern das gesamte Team zählt) aufmerksam. In der neuen Umwelt hängt der Erfolg des Unternehmens im großen Teil von dem Engagement der Mitarbeiter und von der von ihnen erarbeiteten Wertschöpfung ab. Die Firma DHL Express (Poland) nutzt das Leadership Agility-Modell in der täglichen Praxis und bildet dadurch die Voraussetzungen für großartige Ergebnisse nicht nur in Bezug auf

Business-Erfolge sondern auch auf das Menschenkapital. (German) [ABSTRACT FROM AUTHOR]
Wstęp: Zmiany zachodzące współcześnie wymuszają na przedsiębiorstwach postawienie sobie pytania o jakość przywództwa w organizacji i o to czy dotychczasowe działania w tej dziedzinie wspierają sukces firmy. W otoczeniu globalnym przedsiębiorstw zmienia się zarówno struktura społeczna jak i polityczna a nieodwołalne zmiany demograficzne wpływają na rynek bardziej niż kiedykolwiek wcześniej. Aby firmy miały szansę na odniesienie sukcesu w nowym środowisku niezbędne jest więc wprowadzenie nowych paradygmatów przywódczych. Celem pracy było rozpoznanie metod pozwalających na istotną poprawę jakości działania przedsiębiorstwa transportowego. Metody: Badania wykonano na podstawie literaturowej analizy badanego tematu oraz analizy ankiet przesłanych przez pracowników. Wnioski: Model wszechstronności przywódczej (ang. leadership agility) wydaje się być odpowiedzią na pytanie jak przetrwać w nowym świecie.

(continued)

Table 2.2 (continued)

	Koncept leadership agility zwraca uwagę na płynne przechodzenie menadżerów pomiędzy różnymi stylami a także odwrót od przywództwa heroicznego, skupionego na jednej tylko sobie przywódcy na rzecz przywództwa postheroicznego, gdzie liczy się wkład całego zespołu. W nowym środowisku znaczna część sukcesu firmy zależeć będzie od zaangażowania jej pracowników, a co za tym idzie od wartości dodanej jaką wytworzą. DHL Express (Poland) stosuje w codziennej praktyce model wszechstronności przywódczej osiągając dzięki temu nie tylko znakomite wyniki biznesowe ale także te odnoszące się do kapitału ludzkiego. (Polish) [ABSTRACT FROM AUTHOR] Copyright of LogForum is the property of LogForum and its content may not be copied or emailed to multiple sites or posted to a listserv without the copyright holder's express written permission. However, users may print, download, or email articles for individual use. This abstract may be abridged. No warranty is given about the accuracy of the copy. Users should refer to the original published version of the material for the full abstract (Copyright applies to all Abstracts)	

2016	Bennett, J. V., & Murakami, E. T.	Heroic Leadership Redefined in the United States Border Context: Cases Studies of Successful Principals in Arizona and Texas	*International Studies in Educational Administration (Commonwealth Council for Educational Administration & Management [CCEAM])*	This study employs an internationally developed educational leadership theory focused on heroic and post-heroic leadership to analyse school principals in the United States. Heroic leadership is defined as leading in order to generate initiatives for school improvement; post-heroic leadership is defined as encompassing performance and partnership. Successful principals in four schools in high-need areas are analysed. The findings discuss heroic and post-heroic behaviours in relation to: (a) setting directions through heroic and post-heroic leadership models; (b) developing others in relation to teacher leadership, and parental and student involvement; (c) developing an organisational culture; and (d) transforming schools through social justice agendas. [ABSTRACT FROM AUTHOR] Copyright of International Studies in Educational Administration (Commonwealth Council for Educational Administration & Management (CCEAM)) is the property of Commonwealth Council for Educational Administration & Management (CCEAM) and its content may not be copied or emailed to multiple sites or posted to a listserv without the copyright holder's express written permission. However, users may print, download, or email articles for	Journal article	Qualitative	Educational leadership theory

(continued)

Table 2.2 (continued)

				individual use. This abstract may be abridged. No warranty is given about the accuracy of the copy. Users should refer to the original published version of the material for the full abstract (Copyright applies to all Abstracts)			
2018	Coatney, C.	Media rhetoric of post-heroic leadership: Julia Gillard, Barack Obama and Press Gallery journalists, 2010–2013©	*Media International Australia*	Scholars have recognised the Canberra Press Gallery's capacity to contribute to an inclusive, collective style of political leadership in the context of declining nostalgia for heroes of military conflict. While political leaders have signified supporting journalists in a 'cooperative search for truth' about a conflict, the Gallery has influenced these relations as 'the courageous teller of a truth'. This article examines the media rhetoric and Press Gallery relations of Australian Prime Minister Julia Gillard and her identification with US President Barack Obama during the conflict in Afghanistan between 2010 and 2013. Gillard connected to Obama's agenda by arguing, like him, that military sacrifices had been justified because of the need to support marginalised groups, including Afghan women and girls. This article argues that as time went by, Press Gallery journalists increasingly queried and investigated Gillard's rationale for the conflict. The journalists portrayed their role as public defenders of the 'truth' about Australia's military engagement by including Afghanistan sources countering heroic military narratives	Journal article	Qualitative	X

2018	Collinson, M.	What's new about Leadership-as-Practice?	*Leadership*	It appears that leadership studies is now in the throes of a 'new movement', one that, according to its leading exponent, is 'destined to shake the foundations of the very meaning of leadership in the worlds of both theory and practice' (Raelin, 2016b: 1). This 'leading questions' article questions three of Raelin's central claims for this Leadership-as-Practice perspective namely that this approach supersedes other post-heroic perspectives, constitutes a distinct 'movement' and is more radical than critical leadership studies. Arguing that these claims are excessive and have little or no substantial supporting evidence, I suggest that Leadership-as-Practice is better seen as one variant of post-heroic leadership. Furthermore, I contend that the primary weakness of Leadership-as-Practice is its continued lack of critical engagement, particularly in relation to its neglect of asymmetrical power relations and control practices in all their multiple forms	Journal article	Qualitative	Leadership-as-Practice

(continued)

Table 2.2 (continued)

2018	Kelan, E. K., Wratil, P.	Post-heroic Leadership, Tempered Radicalism and Senior Leaders as Change Agents for Gender Equality	*European Management Review*	Micro change agents for gender equality in organisations are often considered to be tempered radicals who work within an existing structure to change the status quo. However for gender equality to happen, it is often claimed that heroic leadership of top leaders, or macro change agents, is required. The aim of this article is to show how CEOs as macro change agents for gender equality can be conceptualised. Drawing on interviews with 20 global CEOs and a literature review, the article develops a framework to conceptualise how CEOs are fostering gender equality around accountability, building ownership, communicating, leading by example, initiating and driving culture change. The article questions the conceptualisation of change agents of gender equality as either tempered radicals, for micro change agents, or heroic leaders, for macro change agents, and argues instead that to be macro change agents for gender equality, CEOs need to display post-heroic leadership and tempered radicalism to foster change in regard to gender relations. © 2017 European Academy of Management	Journal article	Qualitative	X

2018	Koloma Beck, Teresa, Werron, Tobias	Violent Conflictition: Armed Conflicts and Global Competition for Attention and Legitimacy	*International Journal of Politics, Culture, and Society*	The persistence of violence in international politics is often depicted in terms of a gap between the normative ideal of non-violence on the one hand and the actual behavior of governments and other actors on the other. This paper proposes to see this gap as an object of empirical research rather than just as a normative dilemma. We argue that the institutionalization of global norms of non-violence since the mid-to-late nineteenth century has changed the conditions for the reproduction of violent conflicts by embedding local conflicts into global competitions for attention and legitimacy. At the heart of this process, we see a type of observer that we call universalized third parties: international organizations, social scientists, journalists, and similar agents who, by positioning themselves as proponents of universal norms and by objecting violence in the name of humanity, have made violence particularly likely to attract the attention of the so-called world public opinion. This global attention, however, can impact conflicts in different and contradictory ways: On the one hand, violence now is particularly likely to undermine the legitimacy of conflict parties, incenting them to refrain from violence or to try	Journal article	Qualitative	X

(continued)

Table 2.2 (continued)

				to direct attention to the violent behavior of their opponent; on the other hand, violence attracts attention to the conflict, incenting conflict parties to make deliberate use of it in order to call attention to their cause. This complex interplay between local conflicts and global competition is what we call violent conflictition—a neologism coined to indicate the concurrence between conflict and competition			
2018	Körner, Swen, Staller, Mario S.	From system to pedagogy: towards a nonlinear pedagogy of self-defense training in the police and the civilian domain	*Security Journal*	Within public and academic spheres, the question of how civilians and police officers can effectively deal with violent assaults is discussed above all as a question of the "right self-defense system." In the current paper, we advocate for a change from questions of system to questions of pedagogy. Based on the paradigm of nonlinear pedagogy and the underlying theories of complex dynamic systems, we present a model of representative learning design, whose analytical and practical use is presented. We conclude with a discussion of the role of nonlinear pedagogy for the professionalization of self-defense training in the civilian and law enforcement domains	Journal article	Qualitative	Theories of complexity, chaos, and dynamic systems

2018	Ntetha, Siphokazi	A Small Business Case Study of Focused and Distributed Leadership Hybridity in South Africa	Pepperdine University, Graduate School of Education and Psychology	There is convincing evidence that effective leadership is a major contributing factor to small business growth and success. However, attention to leadership focused on founding CEOs abounds at the expense of exploring the distribution of leadership across an organization. This study explored they hybridity of focused and distributed leadership enactment in a fast-growing small business situated in South Africa. The first objective was to form a holistic view of how the members of the organization lead, incorporating leadership focused on key individual leaders and that which is shared and distributed amongst and between others. The second objective was to contextualize leadership hybridity to the South African culture and demands of fast business growth. The third objective was to explore how leaders transform as they navigate the terrains of focused and distributed leadership. The overarching goal was to propose a holistic leadership hybridity framework that appreciates these complexities. A qualitative single case study research design guided the study. The case study database was created from in-depth interviews with leaders and followers, focus group interviews, participant observations of organizational activities, and the review of two documents.	Doctoral dissertation	Qualitative	Theory X, Y and Z

(continued)

Table 2.2 (continued)

				Themes emerged to suggest that there is harmonious leadership hybridity that occurs through both the behaviors of critical individual leaders at the top (notably, the CEO) and those emerging from outside of formal structures through distributed leadership across multiple leadership actors and factors. The South African culture of ubuntu seems to support post-heroic leadership but does not exclude acknowledging that growing a business involves a collection of heroic acts. And lastly, leaders and followers who performed leadership within hybridity (i.e., those that can fluidly move between being a leader or a follower) benefited from enhanced self-regulation, amongst other psychosocial benefits. The insight gained from this study could inform leadership development initiatives that are more effective in growing leaders and small businesses in Southern Africa			
2018	Picard, H., Islam, G.	Free to Do What I Want'? Exploring the ambivalent effects of liberating leadership	*Organization Studies*	This study examines the phenomenon of 'liberating leadership', an emerging trend promising self-mastery and collective unity, resonating with the literature on post-heroic leadership. We evaluate the claims of liberating leadership from a psychodynamic perspective, using a Lacanian approach. We examine how post-heroic forms of leadership reconfigure symbolic and imaginary aspects of follower identification, with ambivalent effects. Drawing empirically on the case of a	Journal article	Qualitative	Leader–follower

				Belgian banking department, we trace how a 'liberating' leader was able to garner intense psychological attachment among followers, accompanied by the 'dark sides' of personal exhaustion and breakdown, normative pressure to be overly happy, and the scapegoating of contrarian managers representing symbolic prohibition			
2019	Ahmad Raza, Bilal Tehreem, Fatima Muhammad Kashif, Imran	Does shared leadership fosters taking charge behaviors? A post-heroic leadership perspective in the public sector higher educational institutes	*Emerald Group Publishing Limited*	Purpose: The purpose of this paper is to advance the theoretical perspective of complexity leadership paradigm to introduce shared leadership style as a precursor of taking charge behavior in public sector higher educational institutions (HEIs) of Pakistan. Moreover, this study unveils the underlying mechanisms of the climate of initiative and psychological safety for clarifying the link of shared leadership and taking charge. Design/methodology/approach: The multi-source and multi-wave data were analyzed by employing double mediation analysis (PROCESS Model 4); using 282 valid responses obtained from a proportionate stratified sample of faculty members working in public sector HEIs of Pakistan. Findings: The result indicates that shared leadership is a suitable style for governing the public sector HEIs and it fosters taking charge behavior in teaching faculty.	Journal article	Quantitative	Complexity Leadership Theory

(continued)

Table 2.2 (continued)

				Additionally, shared leadership creates climates that support initiatives and are psychologically safe that set stage for taking charge behaviors in teaching faculty of public sector HEIs of Pakistan. Originality/value: This research has filled the gap of focusing on more collaborative leadership styles instead of traditional vertical leadership practices in public sector HEIs of Pakistan. Theoretically, this study suggests new insights into the contextual antecedents and mediating mechanisms of taking charge behaviors			
2019	Bilal, Ahmad Raza Fatima, Tehreem Imran, Muhammad Kashif	Does shared leadership fosters taking charge behaviors? A post-heroic leadership perspective in the public sector higher educational institutes	*International Journal of Public Leadership*	Purpose: The purpose of this paper is to advance the theoretical perspective of complexity leadership paradigm to introduce shared leadership style as a precursor of taking charge behavior in public sector higher educational institutions (HEIs) of Pakistan. Moreover, this study unveils the underlying mechanisms of the climate of initiative and psychological safety for clarifying the link of shared leadership and taking charge. Design/methodology/approach: The multi-source and multi-wave data were analyzed by employing double mediation analysis (PROCESS Model 4); using 282 valid responses obtained from a proportionate stratified sample of faculty members working in	Journal article	Quantitative	Complexity Leadership Theory

				public sector HEIs of Pakistan. Findings: The result indicates that shared leadership is a suitable style for governing the public sector HEIs and it fosters taking charge behavior in teaching faculty. Additionally, shared leadership creates climates that support initiatives and are psychologically safe that set stage for taking charge behaviors in teaching faculty of public sector HEIs of Pakistan. Originality/value: This research has filled the gap of focusing on more collaborative leadership styles instead of traditional vertical leadership practices in public sector HEIs of Pakistan. Theoretically, this study suggests new insights into the contextual antecedents and mediating mechanisms of taking charge behaviors			
2019	Bohl, Kenneth W.	Leadership as Phenomenon: Reassessing the Philosophical Ground of Leadership Studies	*Philosophy of Management*	The purpose of this article is to contribute to a more robust theory of leadership that shifts the frame of reference from leadership as exclusively facilitated through a single inspired leader to one that includes the view of leadership as an emergent and complex social phenomenon. The article begins with a review of the leader-centric	Journal article	Qualitative	Leadership theory (leader-centric theories)

(continued)

Table 2.2 (continued)

	approaches that dominated much of twentieth century leadership studies then moves on to present contemporary critiques of leader-centric approaches leading to an alternative perspective of leadership as an emergent and complex social phenomenon. Viewing leadership as an emergent and complex social phenomenon changes our attitude regarding the roles that leaders and others play in the creation of leadership. A central theme of this article is the impact that the concept of emergence has on leadership theory. In response to this changing attitude, the article then moves to return to and reassess the ontological, epistemological and ethical grounds of leadership and concludes that there is an underlying philosophy that supports viewing leadership as an emergent social phenomenon and further suggests that recent work in virtue epistemology along with Calvin Schrag's theory of communicative praxis and transversal rationality, can facilitate a better understanding of leadership as an emergent social phenomenon

2019	Brett, James	Experts and Achievers	*Evolving Digital Leadership*	X	Book chapter	Qualitative	X
2019	Fotaki, Marianna Pullen, Alison	Introducing Affective Embodiment and Diversity	*Diversity, Affect and Embodiment in Organizing*	This occurs against the revelations about the widespread sexual harassment and persisting inequalities in the workplace such as gender pay gap and the absence of women and minoritized others from positions of power. Simultaneously, there has been a powerful backlash against women's empowerment taking the form of anti-gender and postfeminist discourses. We argue that the approach to equal opportunities in the workplace emerging from the liberal, free market conception of employment fails to address the root causes of discrimination because gender and other inequalities are often necessary for sustaining and strengthening the global capital accumulation. This edited collection offers an affective embodiment as a central practice and concept to problematize diversity. Without understanding how embodied differences are conditioned and reproduced, we might be unable to address inequalities in organizations	Book chapter	Qualitative	X

(continued)

Table 2.2 (continued)

2019	Ghin, Peter P.	The Sick Body: Conceptualizing the Experience of Illness in Senior Leadership	*Diversity, Affect and Embodiment in Organizing*	There has been a proliferation of research that has explored the role of embodiment in leadership; however, a common feature of this literature is the assumption of 'corporeal intactness', that is, leaders' bodies are treated as unfailingly healthy objects. Ghin suggests that this absence reflects a broader oversight in leadership scholarship to countenance the illness experience of those in formal positions of organizational power. He argues that the conceptualization of a 'sick body' challenges individualistic, masculine, and heroic characterizations of leadership, which have been stubbornly resistant to change and further emboldened by health discourses and practices that promote body mastery. Revealing the sick-bodied leader enables a different leadership discourse to emerge, one that recognizes the universality of the illness experience and ordinariness of leaders' bodies	Book chapter	Qualitative	X

2019	Just, S. N. Louise Muhr, S.	"Together we rise": Collaboration and contestation as narrative drivers of the Women's March	*Leadership*	The Women's March is arguably the most important counter-narrative to Trump's post-truth regime, but does it also present a leadership alternative to his populist and authoritarian style? And is this alternative necessarily better than currently dominant social formations? In this paper, we argue that the Women's March is partially configured by similar forces of affective circulation as those governing pro-Trump narratives, but that it is different and better in one important respect. The narratives of the Women's March are driven by both collaboration and contestation, meaning its circulation is both centripetal and centrifugal. We substantiate this claim through a close reading of the narration of the Women's March–from its inception until its first anniversary. Here, we focus particularly on the development from a moment of resistance to a political movement, arguing that this process offers a prototype for conceptualizing a new form of "rebel" or social movement leadership. Hence, the Women's March not only offers a different and better alternative to the leadership of Trump but also an opportunity for promoting and refining leadership theory in the post-heroic vein. © The Author(s) 2018	Journal article	Qualitative	Leadership of the Women's March

(continued)

Table 2.2 (continued)

2019	Koivunen, Niina, Parush, Tamar	Using Choir Conducting to Improve Leadership Practice	*Sensuous Learning for Practical Judgment in Professional Practice: Volume 1: Arts-based Methods*	The authors examine art-based workshops that are designed and facilitated by Danish choir conductor Peter Hanke, aimed at improving the leadership skills of business managers. The participants are taught the basics of conducting, invited to conduct a small professional choir, and receive feedback on their performance. The process of learning leadership is based on two mechanisms: analogically mediated inquiry and embodied performance. Participants also learn to view leadership as a balancing act between traditional, authoritative forms of leadership and new egalitarian, post-heroic forms	Book chapter	Qualitative	Social constructionism
2019	Onyura, Betty, Crann, Sara, Tannenbaum, David Whittaker, Mary Kay, Murdoch, Stuart, Freeman, Risa	Is postgraduate leadership education a match for the wicked problems of health systems leadership? A critical systematic review	*Perspectives on Medical Education*	There have been a growing number of leadership education programs for physicians. However, debates about the value and efficacy of leadership education in medicine persist, and there are calls for systematic and critical perspectives on medical leadership development. Here, we review evidence on postgraduate leadership education and discuss findings in relation to contemporary evidence on leadership education and practice	Journal article	Qualitative	X

2019	Openo, J.	Can (Post-heroic) leadership be taught (Online)? A library educator's expansion of Baldwin, Ching, and Friesen's grounded theory model of online course design and development	*Journal of Education for Library and Information Science*	Many Master of Library and Information Science (MLIS) programs are now offered online, and most of these programs offer courses on leadership and management principles. Teaching leadership in any context presents challenges because leadership is a hazy and confounding concept. The intrinsic problems in teaching leadership are compounded by the professional context of libraries; librarianship is a feminized profession whereas being a leader is often a male-oriented construct. This confounding mix of teaching leadership informed by feminist theory is magnified by the challenge of teaching online, where the harassment of women academics (such as MIT's Chris Bourg) is pervasive and destructive. There is a paucity of research and discussion on how to design online leadership courses in graduate MLIS programs that account for these challenges. This paper contributes to this discussion by expanding upon Baldwin, Ching, and Friesen's grounded theory model of online course design and development. Grounded theory is an experiential methodology, and this paper aligns with Baldwin et al.'s grounded theory approach by applying constant	Journal article	Qualitative	X

(continued)

Table 2.2 (continued)

				comparison between the author's experience designing an online graduate-level leadership course and their model. © Journal of Education for Library and Information Science 2019			
2019	Pan, Hui-Ling Wendy, Nyeu, Fong-Yee	Changing Practices of School Leadership in Taiwan: Evolving Education Reforms	*Perspectives on School Leadership in Asia Pacific Contexts*	For the past three decades, the Taiwanese education system has undergone waves of reform and gradual deregulation beginning with the lifting of the martial law in 1987. A more democratic and open society opened up new ideas for education and school management. These reforms have greatly influenced the content of education, the organization and power structure of education, the roles of teachers and principals, and very importantly how principals lead and schools are managed. This chapter examines the education reforms in Taiwan throughout the years in terms of its impact, and the challenges they pose to leadership in schools	Book chapter	Qualitative	X
2019	Seale, Oliver	Re-imagining Leadership Development for Middle-level Academic Leaders in Africa	*Journal of Higher Education in Africa/Revue de l'enseignement supérieur en Afrique*	[The university today is a postmodern, neo-liberal, competitive, boundary-less knowledge conglomerate, a far cry from its historical, traditional, classical and collegial roots. Although remaining true to its primary mission of research, teaching and community engagement, its organisational form has changed significantly, with its concomitant implications for governance, leadership and management, especially in a	Journal article	Qualitative	Theorisation on leadership development for academic leaders

	developing world context. The regional and institutional disruptions and protests by students and other stakeholders in African countries like Algeria, Kenya, Sudan and, more recently, South Africa in the guise of the '#RhodesMustFall,' '#FeesMustFall' and '#OpenStellenbosch' campaigns, starkly illustrates this challenging, nebulous environment of higher education on the continent. The article provides a reflection and engagement on these critical issues and aims to illustrate that: (i) the global and local contexts of higher education have changed dramatically, with its concomitant added levels of complexity for academic leaders; (ii) this environment has implications for the conception and practice of leadership and management in universities, for middle level academic leaders in particular; and (iii) this setting provides the backdrop for a holistic and integrated academic leadership intervention in universities in Africa. L'université est aujourd'hui un conglomérat de connaissances1 postmoderne, néolibéral, compétitif et sans frontières, loin de ses racines historiques, traditionnelles, classiques et collégiales. Bien qu'elle reste fidèle à sa mission principale de recherche, d'enseignement et d'engagement communautaire, sa forme	

(continued)

Table 2.2 (continued)

		organisationnelle a considérablement changé, avec des *implications* concomitantes de gouvernance, de leadership et de gestion, en particulier dans un monde en développement. Les perturbations et protestations régionales et institutionnelles d'étudiants et d'autres parties prenantes de pays africains comme l'Algérie, le Kenya, le Soudan et, plus récemment, l'Afrique du Sud avec des campagnes comme #RhodesMustFall, #FeesMustFall et #OpenStellenbosch illustrent clairement cet environnement nébuleux et difficile de l'enseignement supérieur sur le continent. L'article fournit une réflexion et un engagement sur ces questions importantes et tente d'illustrer que: (i) les contextes, mondial et local, de l'enseignement supérieur ont changé de façon spectaculaire avec des niveaux supplémentaires et concomitants de complexité pour les responsables universitaires; (ii) cet environnement a des implications pour les universités, dans la conception et la pratique du leadership et de la gestion de niveau intermédiaires en particulier les dirigeants; et (iii) ce cadre fournit la toile de fond pour une intervention de leadership académique holistique et intégrée dans les universités en Afrique]

2019	Sobral, F. Furtado, L.	Post-heroic leadership: Current trends and challenges for leadership education	*RAE Revista de Adminis-tracao de Empresas*	The dominant leadership paradigm of the industrial era views the leader as a hero: an active subject, who visualizes the future, defines and communicates the strategy, inspires and motivates those who are led, assigns roles, and evaluates and rewards according to performance. Followers, on the other hand, are seen as reactive, malleable, and moldable individuals. The most prominent theories arising from this paradigm include charismatic, transformational, transactional, and visionary leadership. Although these theories have their specificities, they all consider leadership as a unidirectional, top-down influencing process, and draw a clear line of separation between leaders and followers. Here, Sobral and Furtado present some new perspectives that guide the studies on leadership within the paradigm of post-heroic leadership, in order to contribute to the consolidation and deepening of a new concept of leadership in Brazil. They challenge the traditional view of leadership as a vertical, hierarchical phenomenon and monopoly of power or authority and identify the main barriers that hinder the training and development of post-heroic leaders	Journal article	Qualitative	Leader–follower

(continued)

Table 2.2 (continued)

2020	Abson, Emma	Exploring Relational Connections and the Emergence of Shared Leadership in Experiential Agencies	Sheffield Hallam University (United Kingdom)	This exploratory and cross-sectional study focussed on the specific setting of experiential event agencies and explored leadership through the lens of the 'post-heroic' leadership theories, in particular the theory of shared leadership. Adopting a social constructionist perspective, the investigation took the form of a collective case study, using a constructionist grounded theory approach to guide the data collection, analysis and theory development. The research explores the way in which leadership is shared among team members within three experiential event agencies. Despite the growing body of research which indicates that shared leadership has a positive effect on team performance and team effectiveness, there has yet to have been any research that explores the conditions which enable shared leadership to be practiced in the context of cross functional, interdependent, project based teams such as those found in experiential agencies. This, coupled with the lack of empirical research around the form and function of the leadership within the event industry, forms the background to this research. This thesis addresses these gaps in knowledge by identifying which conditions of work enable shared leadership to become a useful process in project based event organisations. The study therefore responds to the following overarching	Doctoral dissertation	Qualitative	Theory of shared leadership

question: 'How is leadership shared in an experiential agency?' The analysis of the data collected from the three case studies resulted in the emergence of a new theory of relational connections and the emergence of shared leadership. The theory suggests that shared leadership develops through relational connections within organisations, and demonstrates that the relationships between individuals within these organisations are the cornerstone of effective participation in shared leadership. This research is the first to closely examine the nature of workplace 5 relationships in the context of shared leadership and, in particular, it has illuminated how these connections are constructed through a sense of belonging in the workplace and trust between team members. The developed theory therefore reveals the dynamics that underpin shared leadership and gives a clear understanding of how these relational connections are constructed. In doing so, it indicates that shared leadership is an influence process that emerges from interactions, and resides in the relationships that exist in work groups. This study has therefore engaged with the complex–and topical–problems of how shared leadership emerges and the processes of leadership within

(continued)

Table 2.2 (continued)

				experiential agencies, and has provided new empirical material which is important from both theoretical and practical perspectives			
2020	Campbell, Louise	Organisation Ethics, Relational Leadership and Nursing	*Nursing Ethics: Feminist Perspectives*	The purpose of this chapter is to explore the relevance of the concept of relational leadership for nurses. Leadership is an issue which has received increased attention within the field of organisation ethics over the course of the past two decades. Organisation ethics is the study of the ethical issues which arise in the context of managing and running complex organisations, such as healthcare organisations. Decisions made by managers and executives within healthcare organisations have a fundamental impact on the working conditions of nurses and other clinical staff, and may compromise their ability to care for patients as they would wish to. The challenges involved in balancing the requirements of the organisation with the needs of individual patients may result in moral distress for nurses and other healthcare professionals. Relational leadership reconceptualises leadership, not as a hierarchical relationship between 'leaders' and 'followers', but in terms of a set of 'relational practices' or competencies which blur the distinction between leaders and followers. Relational leadership recognises that acts of leadership occur at every level within an organisation and it empowers	Book chapter	Qualitative	Relational leadership

				those with less organisational influence to lead in situations in which their expertise is required and to challenge existing leadership structures which undermine the quality of their work. Developing the relational competencies which are a prerequisite of relational leadership may transform nurses' understanding of their own agency and revolutionise their experience of the work they do			
2020	Ciulla, Joanne B.	Afterword	*The Search for Ethics in Leadership, Business, and Beyond*	X	Book chapter	Qualitative	X
2020	Ciulla, Joanne B.	Ethics and Effectiveness: The Nature of Good Leadership	*The Search for Ethics in Leadership, Business, and Beyond*	In 1995, I published "Leadership Ethics, Mapping the Territory" in the Business Ethics Quarterly (5.1, 7–28). The article critically examined the literature in leadership studies and then laid out some of the key problems and parameters for a field of leadership ethics. I imagined a field of study that was analogous to other areas of applied ethics, such as business or medical ethics. The literature in leadership ethics would be multidisciplinary and interdisciplinary, and draw from work in philosophy, the sciences, social sciences, and all of the humanities. It would take into account and be integrated with other areas of research in leadership studies. One of the key	Book chapter	Qualitative	X

(continued)

Table 2.2 (continued)

		objectives in leadership studies is to understand what makes a leader effective. The role of leader is unique in that a leader's competence or incompetence potentially benefits or harms others. From an ethical point of view, being an ethical, incompetent, leader can be just as bad as being a competent, unethical leader. Hence, I have argued that the overarching challenge of leadership, and the framework for leadership ethics, is understanding and navigating the relationship between ethics and effectiveness. This framework also offers a clear and simple way of describing and assessing good leaders – a good leader is both ethical and effective. This chapter is the longest in the book because it elaborates on the ethical challenges that make it difficult for leaders to be ethical and effective. It places these challenges in the context of the leadership literature, and it talks about everything from the personal challenges of self-interest and power, to the problem related to dirty hands and moral luck

2020	Harter, Nathan W., Heuvel, Sean M.	New Perspectives on Heroic/Post-heroic Leadership and on Heroic Followership	*International Leadership Journal*	This article challenges the concept of post-heroic leadership and offers new perspectives about the term and its role within the leadership studies discipline. It also provides insights about the origins and evolution of heroic leadership and argues that instead of post-heroic leadership, scholars should look to refine the notion of heroism in leadership and use a more fitting vocabulary. The article then closes with a brief case study of Admiral Lord Horatio Nelson, a classic "hero-leader," who upon closer examination, displayed many attributes of a connective leader. [ABSTRACT FROM AUTHOR] Copyright of International Leadership Journal is the property of TST, Inc. and its content may not be copied or emailed to multiple sites or posted to a listserv without the copyright holder's express written permission. However, users may print, download, or email articles for individual use. This abstract may be abridged. No warranty is given about the accuracy of the copy. Users should refer to the original published version of the material for the full abstract (Copyright applies to all Abstracts)	Journal article	Qualitative	Post-heroic leadership

(continued)

Table 2.2 (continued)

2020	Ropo, A., Mäkinen, E. I., Seppä, I.	Online company blogs as narrations of plural leadership	*Journal of Organizational Change Management*	Purpose: The purpose of this paper is to examine how companies that characterise their leadership style as plural, shared or distributed narrate their actions and practices in online blog texts. Design/methodology/approach: The data consist of online blog texts published by seven Finnish IT companies. The analytical strategy draws on both thematic and structural approach to narrative analysis. The blog texts were analysed thematically to uncover different aspects of plural leadership. The analysis revealed a narrative pattern consisting of three categories that explain why and how companies implemented plural leadership. Findings: The first category in the narrative pattern describes the motivation for engaging in plural leadership. The second category explains how the companies broke down existing hierarchies in order to create new flexible work roles. The third category describes how the organisations sought to create a communal culture and a strong sense of trust using symbols, material objects and spaces. Research limitations/implications: The study contributes to leadership research that emphasises post-heroic leadership conceptualisations. The narrative pattern provides future empirical	Journal article	Qualitative	Plurality of leadership

	studies a framework for analysing plural leadership practices in different organisational settings. Whereas this study sheds light on the ways in which organisations and their leadership practices can be investigated using online data, traditional organisational ethnographies can make a further contribution to this line of research. Practical implications: Implementing plural leadership in organisations can lead to informal power plays. Attention should be paid on to how plural leadership evolves in flat hierarchies and promotes community building. Originality/value: Company webpages have rich information on how companies operate and perceive themselves. They provide yet another window for observing organisational activities. This study makes a novel contribution to how plural leadership is practiced and conceptualised in online blog texts. © 2019, Emerald Publishing Limited	

(continued)

Table 2.2 (continued)

2020	Ryömä, A.	The interplay of heroic and post-heroic leadership: Exploring tensions in leadership manifestations in the oscillations between onstage and offstage contexts	*Scandinavian Journal of Management*	This paper strives to extend knowledge about tensions in heroic and post-heroic leadership. Previous studies have focused on one overarching context rather than explained how these tensions interplay in diverse contextual circumstances. This paper adopts a Goffmanian perspective and explores the tensions between heroic and post-heroic leadership in onstage and offstage contexts. By drawing on semi-structured interviews and an ethnographic observation of ice hockey teams, the paper proposes three dynamics by which these tensions are manifested in offstage and onstage contexts, namely: 'Coaching over-the-others', 'Starring up-to-the-others', and 'Doing self in-the-others'. The paper concludes by discussing the importance of looking at the dynamics by which tensions between heroic and post-heroic leadership are manifested in multiple circumstances of team leadership. © 2019 The Author	Journal article	Qualitative	Goffmanian perspective

Column 2	*Column 3*	*Method*	*Sample*	*Column 5*	*Temporal perspective*	*Levels of analysis (coding: Multi-level, single level, dyadic)*	*Settings (e.g., health care, education, for-profit organizations)*
X	X	Standpoint	X	X	X	X	X
X	X	X	X	X	X	X	X
X	X	Review	X	X	1980s	X	X
X	X	X	X	X	X	X	X
X	X	Review	X	X	X	X	X
X	X	?	48 IT companies—dyads of project managers and their subordinates	X	Years 1995–1996	Dyadic	IT
X	X	Review	X	X	X	X	X
X	X	In-depth interviews, formal and informall follow-ups, observations, notes	5 women	X	Period 2000–2002	Single level	Education
X	X	Observations, surveys, secondary data, triangulation	9 mid-level work teams	X	5-month period	Single level	Manufacturing
X	X	Narrative (story)	X	X	X	X	X
X	X	Review (viewpoint), interviews	6 women from quliting group of professionals or middle class	X	X	Single level	Textile (quliting)

(continued)

Table 2.2 (continued)

X	X	Case studies, *within* and cross-case analysis, interviews, documents, observations	10 women *administrators* in accredited architecture programs, departments, schools, and colleges within American colleges and universities	X	Year 2007	Single level	Architecture
X	X	Case study	140 senior—and more junior-positioned employees at general FE colleges	X	2.5 year period between 2004 and 2006	Single level	Education
X	X	Ethnographic observations, interviews	11 persons working on the film	5 condustors and 5 concert hall personnel members	2–3-year period	Single level	Arts
X	X	Review	X	X	20+ years	X	Education
X	X	Review	X	X	X	X	X
X	X	Experience	More than 50 women	X	10-year period	Single level	X
X	X	Framework development (competency framework)	X	X	X	X	X
X	X	X	X	X	X	X	X
X	X	X	X	X	X	X	X

X	X	Observations	2184 matches	25 teams	12 years	Multi-level	Sports (Norwegian premium league—football)
X	X	X	X	X	X	X	X
X	X	Case study	24 students, allies, community activists, heads of non-profit organizations, and service	X	Year 2006	Single level	X
X	X	Framework development	X	X	X	X	X
X	X	Inquiry, storytelling	4 women from the non-profit organization (author +3)	X	6 months	Single level	Non-profit organisations
Mundane managerial leadership	X	Interviews, formal and informal observations, illustrative cases, viewpoint	Mid-level and senior managers (no other information)	X	X	Single level	X
X	X	X	X	X	X	X	X
X	X	In-depth interviews	17 Canadian corporate directors	X	One-time study	Single level	X
X	X	Case study (longitudinal), meetings, observations, secondary data	X	X	18 months	Single level	Human resources (recruitement)

(continued)

Table 2.2 (continued)

X	X	Case studies (multiple perspectives), semi-structured individual and group interviews with principals, teachers, students, parents and school board members, document search	X	X	X	Single level	Education
X	X	Workshops, semi-structured interviews, secondary data	9 Hanke's workshops	X	Years 2008–2012	Single level	Diverse industries
X	X	Review	X	X	X	X	X
X	X	Interviews, cross-caes analysis	8 nurse and physician co-leaders	X	Year 2006	Multi-level	Health care
X	X	Interviews	35 key personnel from organisations with responsibility for national co-ordination, education, and membership services (the chair, a new board member and the CEO)	X	Year 2011	Single level	Sports (outdoor activity sector)
X	X	Standpoint	X	X	X	X	X
X	X	Novel (fiction) writing	X	X	X	X	Arts

X	X	Ethnographic observations, social media observation, semi-structured interviews	10 protestors	X	2 weeks	Single level	Politics
X	X	Review	X	X	X	X	Education
X	X	Review, questionnaire	Interviews—no information with whom	X	X	Single level	Transport
X	X	Case studies, semi-structured interviews	37 participants in Arizona	X	X	Single level	Education
X	X	Secondary data (keywords, speeches, press conferences)	212 articles during Gillard's prime ministership from 20 June 2010 to 26 June 2013	X	Period 2010–2013	Single level	Media, politics
X	X	Review	X	X	X	X	X
X	X	Interviews, literature review	20 global CEOs (5 women, 15 men)	X	X	Single level	Diverse industries
X	X	X	X	X	X	X	X
X	X	X	X	X	X	X	X
X	X	Case study, in-depth interviews, observations, documents' review	17 participants (11 interviewees—5 leaders and 6 followers—and 2 focus groups)	X	Year 2018	Single level	Fast-growing businesses

(continued)

Table 2.2 (continued)

X	X	Case study (*in*-depth interviews, observations, archival data)	26 departmental members (middle- or top-level managers, sales representatives, administrative assistants, analysts) and higher-up officials and senior managers within the bank	X	Two-wave (2011)	Multi-level	Banking
X	X	Questionnaire	282 faculty members working in public sector HEIs of Pakistan	X	Three-wave data collection (one year)	Single level	Education
X	X	Questionnaire	282 valid responses obtained from a proportionate stratified sample of faculty members working in public sector HEIs of Pakistan	X	Three-wave data collection (one year)	Single level	Education
X	X	Review and critique	X	X	X	X	X
X	X	X	X	X	X	X	X
X	X	Editorial	X	X	X	X	X
X	X	Review	X	X	X	X	X
X	X	Article, narratives, other sources	X	X	Year 2018	X	Politics

X	X	Observations (workshops, interviews, feedback materials, writings, website, blog); semi-structured interviews	9 workshops with 20–25 managers	X	Years 2009–2010	Single level	Diverse industries (financial firms, media, communication, management consulting)
X	X	Review and critique	31 studies represented five countries across three continents	X	10-year period (2007–2017)	X	Health care
X	X	Review, course development (practically-oriented)	X	X	X	X	Education
X	X	Review	X	X	X	X	Education
X	X	Framework development, review, secondary data interviews, triangulation	26 deans (of whom 10 were women), their line managers, human resource managers and other key informants at six universities in the Gauteng province, South Africa	X	X	Single level	Education
X	X	Essay	X	X	X	X	X
Theory of relational connections	The emergence of shared leadership	Semi-structured interviews, observation and documentation analysis	All layers of management hierarchy and employees from across the business	X	Year-long period	Single level	For-profit organisation (event management and agencies)

(continued)

Table 2.2 (continued)

X	X	Review	X	X	X	X	Health care
X	X	X	X	X	X	X	X
X	X	X	X	X	X	X	X
X	X	Review and critique	X	X	X	X	X
X	X	Conceptual, reality construction, narration	89 online blog texts that had been published by seven Finnish IT companies in the Spring and Summer of 2017	X	Year 2017	Multi-level	IT
X	X	Semi-structured interviews, ethnographic observation	18 informants (8 head coaches and 10 players)	X	Years 2008–2011	Single level	Sports (ice hockey teams)

References

Aaltio-Marjosola, I., & Takala, T. (2000). Charismatic leadership, manipulation and the complexity of organizational life. *Journal of Workplace Learning, 12*, 146–158.

Allison, S. T., & Goethals, G. R. (2013). *Heroic leadership: An influence taxonomy of 100 exceptional individuals*. Routledge.

Badaracco, J. L. (2002). *Leading quietly: An unorthodox guide to doing the right thing*. Harvard Business School Press.

Barbuto, J. E., Jr., & Wheeler, D. W. (2006). Scale development and construct clarification of servant leadership. *Group & Organization Management, 31*(3), 300–326.

Block, P. (1993). *Stewardship: Choosing service over self-interest*. Berrett-Koehler.

Bodla, A. A., Tang, N., Van Dick, R., & Mir, U. R. (2019). Authoritarian leadership, organizational citizenship behavior, and organizational deviance. *Leadership & Organization Development Journal, 40*, 583–599.

Bradford, D. L., & Cohen, A. R. (1998). *Power up: Transforming organizations through shared leadership*. Wiley.

Cheng, J. T., Anderson, C., Tenney, E. R., Brion, S., Moore, D. A., & Logg, J. M. (2020). The social transmission of overconfidence. *Journal of Experimental Psychology: General, 150*, 157–186.

Conger, J. A. (1989). Leadership: The art of empowering others. *Academy of Management Perspectives, 3*(1), 17–24.

Conger, J. A., Kanungo, R. N., & Menon, S. T. (2000). Charismatic leadership and follower effects. *Journal of Organizational Behavior, 21*(7), 747–767.

Drath, W. (2001). *The deep blue sea: Rethinking the source of leadership*. Jossey-Bass.

Ferris, G. R., Liden, R. C., Munyon, T. P., Summers, J. K., Basik, K. J., & Buckley, M. R. (2009). Relationships at work: Toward a multidimensional conceptualization of dyadic work relationships. *Journal of Management, 35*(6), 1379–1403.

Fletcher, J. K. (2004). The paradox of postheroic leadership: An essay on gender, power, and transformational change. *The Leadership Quarterly, 15*(5), 647–661.

Follett, M. P. (1924). *Creative experience*. Longmans Green.

Galunic, C. (2020). *Backstage leadership: The invisible work of highly effective leaders*. Palgrave Macmillan.

George, J. M. (2000). Emotions and leadership: The role of emotional intelligence. *Human Relations, 53*(8), 1027–1055.

Greenleaf, R. K. (1977). *Servant Leadership*. Jossey-Bass.

Greenleaf, R. K. (1996). *On becoming a servant-leader*. Jossey-Bass.

Greenleaf, R. K. (1998). *The power of servant leadership*. Berrett-Koehler Publishers Inc.

Groysberg, B. (2010). *Chasing stars: The myth of talent and the portability of performance* (1st ed.). Princeton University Press.
Gu, J., Wang, G., Liu, H., Song, D., & He, C. (2018). Linking authoritarian leadership to employee creativity. *Chinese Management Studies, 12*, 384–406.
Halpin, A. W., & Croft, D. B. (1963). *The organizational climate of schools*. Midwest Administration Center.
Hannah, S. T., Sumanth, J. J., Lester, P., & Cavarretta, F. (2014). Debunking the false dichotomy of leadership idealism and pragmatism: Critical evaluation and support of newer genre leadership theories. *Journal of Organizational Behavior, 35*(5), 598–621.
Harrington, M. (2000). *Care and equality*. Routledge.
Harter, J., Schmidt, F., & Hayes, T. (2002). Business-unit-level relationship between employee satisfaction, employee engagement, and business outcomes: A meta-analysis. *The Journal of Applied Psychology, 87*, 268–279.
Hosking, D., Dachler, H. P., & Gergen, K. J. (1995). *Management and organization: Relational alternative to individualism*. Ashgate Publishing.
Kaeufer, K., Scharmer, C. O., & Versteegen, U. (2003). *Reinventing the Health Care System from Within: The Case of a Regional Physician Network in Germany* (MIT Workplace Center Working Paper #WPC0006).
Kiazad, K., Restubog, S. L. D., Zagenczyk, T. J., Kiewitz, C., & Tang, R. L. (2010). In pursuit of power: The role of authoritarian leadership in the relationship between supervisors' Machiavellianism and subordinates' perceptions of abusive supervisory behavior. *Journal of Research in Personality, 44*(4), 512–519.
Konczak, L., Stelly, D., & Trusty, M. (2000). Defining and measuring empowering leader behaviors: Development of an upward feedback instrument. *Educational and Psychological Measurement, 60*, 301–313.
Kouzes, J. M., & Posner, B. Z. (2003). *The leadership challenge* (3rd ed.). Wiley.
Kruger, J., & Dunning, D. (1999). Unskilled and unaware of it: How difficulties in recognizing one's own incompetence lead to inflated self-assessments. *Journal of Personality and Social Psychology, 77*(6), 1121–1134.
Laub, J. A. (1999). *Assessing the servant organization Development of the Servant Organizational Leadership Assessment (SOLA) Instrument* (Doctor of Education). Florida Atlantic University, Boca Raton, FL.
Li, Y., & Sun, J.-M. (2015). Traditional Chinese leadership and employee voice behavior: A cross-level examination. *The Leadership Quarterly, 26*(2), 172–189.
Lipman Blumen, J. (1996). *The connective edge*. Jossey-Bass.
Lipnack, J., & Stamps, J. (2000). *Virtual teams: People working across boundaries with technology*. Wiley.

Luthans, F., Avolio, B., Cameron, K. S., Dutton, J., & Quinn, R. E. (2003). Authentic leadership: A positive developmental approach. *Positive Organizational Scholarship*, 241–261.

McCullough, M. E., Hoyt, W. T., & Rachal, K. C. (2000). What we know (and need to know) about assessing forgiveness constructs. *Forgiveness: Theory, research, and practice* (pp. 65–88). Guilford Press.

McIntosh, P. (1989). *Feeling like a fraud, Part 2* (Working Paper #37). Centers for Women. Available from Centers for Women, Wellesley College.

Morrison, E. W., & Milliken, F. J. (2000). Organizational silence: A barrier to change and development in a pluralistic world. *Academy of Management Review*, *25*(4), 706–725.

Patterson, K. (2003). *Servant leadership: A theoretical model* (p. 64). Dissertation Abstracts International.

Pearce, C. L., & Conger, J. A. (2002). *Shared leadership: Reframing the hows and whys of leadership*. Sage.

Pearce, C. L., & Conger, J. A. (2003). *Shared leadership: Reframing the hows and whys of leadership*. Sage.

Pearce, C. L., & Sims Jr, H. P. (2000). Shared leadership: Toward a multi-level theory of leadership. *Advances in Interdisciplinary Studies of Work Teams, 7*, 115–139.

Perlow, L. (2003). *When you say yes but mean no: How silencing conflict wrecks relationships and companies*. Crown Publishing.

Peterson, C., & Seligman, M. E. P. (2004). *Character strengths and virtues: A handbook and classification*. Oxford University Press.

Ronay, R., Oostrom, J. K., Lehmann-Willenbrock, N., Mayoral, S., & Rusch, H. (2019). Playing the trump card: Why we select overconfident leaders and why it matters. *The Leadership Quarterly*, *30*(6), 101316.

Russell, R., & Stone, A. (2002). A review of servant leadership attributes: Developing a practical model. *Leadership & Organization Development Journal, 23*, 145–157.

Seely Brown, J., & Duguid, P. (2000). *The social life of information*. Harvard Business School Press.

Senge, P., & Kaeufer, K. (2001). Communities of leaders or no leadership at all. *Management, 21C*, 186–204.

Spears, R. (1995). Editorial. *British Journal of Social Psychology, 34*(2), 125–125.

Stone, A., Russell, R., & Patterson, K. (2004). Transformational versus servant leadership: A difference in leader focus. *Leadership & Organization Development Journal, 25*, 349–361.

Thompson, L. L. (2000). *Making the team: A guide for managers*. Prentice hall.

Useem, M. (2001). *Leading up*. Crown Business.

van Dierendonck, D. (2010). Servant leadership: A review and synthesis. *Journal of Management, 37*(4), 1228–1261.

Wilson, S. M., & Ferch, S. R. (2005). Enhancing resilience in the workplace through the practice of caring relationships. *Organization Development Journal, 23*(4), 45–60.
Yukl, G. A. (1998). *Leadership in organizations* (4th ed.). Prentice Hall.

CHAPTER 3

Post-Heroic Leadership in the Context of Humanizing Hybrid Work

Abstract The future of work is quickly shifting, and hybrid work is bound to become the prevailing form on a global level. Post-heroic leadership behaviours can help establish an environment in which remote and hybrid workers can flourish, as leading people from a distance demands a different skill set from both leaders and followers. Currently, there is strong desire for flexible work policies, developing new approaches to work arrangements and designing the offices of tomorrow. However, combining remote and onsite work can mean stress and overwork. A brief history of management thought is presented, arguing for the importance of post-heroic leaders to humanize hybrid work by emphasizing meaning and trust.

Keywords Hybrid work · Algorithmic management · Humanizing work · Future of work · Work from anywhere

3.1 The Rise of Hybrid Work

A change in the way we work on a global scale is happening before our eyes. The future of modern work is quite likely going to be hybrid and there is a mounting body of research dealing with the matter (Choudhury, 2020; Fayard et al., 2021; Gratton, 2021; Halford, 2005). Some work

M. Škerlavaj, *Post-Heroic Leadership*,
https://doi.org/10.1007/978-3-030-90820-1_3

will be done in the office, some at home, and some from anywhere. We are not referring to the gig workers (Petriglieri et al., 2018) or digital nomads alone (Woldoff & Litchfield, 2021). A change in how we work is happening and is here to stay. In this chapter, we would like to emphasize that post-heroic leadership behaviours should be even more salient in such a work context.

Along with the practice of working from home, research on the possible future of work has clearly gained explosive acceleration. The recent joint publication of 29 world-renowned organizational psychologists (Kniffin et al., 2021) brings about some lessons the field offers about the future of work. The authors particularly emphasize that leading people one does not see requires modern approaches towards leadership that are building upon the sense of autonomy, mastery, and purpose. They also warn that social distancing increases feelings of loneliness, burnout, presenteeism, and the risk of workaholism. It is interesting to note that in virtual teamwork we lack in-depth communication, but that people are actually more willing to help each other.

Researchers (Kniffin et al., 2021) find that the times of the COVID-19 pandemic are also the times of deepening social and economic disparities. For both individuals and their families, the segment of the workforce to which they belong is now even more telling. The difference in being a worker from home, a key talent, on hold, or maybe even without a job has real meaning. Even from an organizational point of view, the cards have been reshuffled. Some industries are undergoing fundamental changes, in others, earlier trends have accelerated, and still others are discovering newer and newer opportunities.

Dingel and Neiman (2020) tried to estimate the extent of work that can be done from home in the long run. They discovered that this percentage in the 85 countries involved depends on the overall development of the country; for the USA, the number was 37% and for Slovenia 38%. The differences between industries are enormous. At the top of the chart are computing (one hundred percent), finance and insurance (92), education (85), law and management (84). At the bottom, there are construction, food, maintenance, manufacturing, agriculture, logistics, and health care (from zero to three percent). Jobs that can be done from anywhere (regardless of location) are also better paid and performed by more educated people with generally more flexible psychological profiles.

Consistent with these findings, the April 2020 Gartner study also finds that 41% of employees report that they would like to work from home at least occasionally in the future. Spataro (2020) has apparently covered a slightly more service sector, with as many as 82% of managers wanting more flexible work policies for working from home, and 71% of employees and managers wanting to be able to continue working from home at least occasionally. Research (Aleksić & Černe, 2020) and experience in some organizations also show that the desire for more flexible forms of work is very much present. The distribution among those who want to work only from home, partly from home, or exclusively at work is one-third for each (Aleksić et al., 2020).

There are several lessons learnt thus far on how to approach hybrid work. Gratton (2021) for instance argues that when designing flexible work arrangements leaders need to focus on individual human concerns, not just institutional ones. She also claims that the challenge of redesigning the work model from the traditional 9-to-5 office to the anywhere-anytime model requires focusing on jobs and tasks, projects and workflows, as well as employee preferences along with inclusion and fairness simultaneously. Fayard et al. (2021) emphasize the need to redesign the office of tomorrow so that it will be designed for human moments. They see the office performing three major functions—social anchor, schoolhouse, and a hub for unstructured collaboration. All those are major considerations for shared and servant types of leadership, together forming the post-heroic leadership.

We also realized, of course, that both remote and hybrid work comes at a price. Neuroscientist Spataro (2020) reports on his experiments using brainwave images on the electroencephalogram (EEG). The images show that for tasks in the virtual environment one activates significantly more brain patterns associated with stress and overwork compared to the same tasks performed outside of the virtual environment. Specifically, high levels of saturation begin to appear after 30 to 40 min of video sessions and excessive levels of stress after two hours. The causes are a constant focus on the screen, a lack of nonverbal cues, a lack of overview of the people we interact with. Research construct named "Zoom fatigue" became a part of the popular vocabulary (Bailenson, 2021; Fossilien & Duff, 2020; Morris, 2020).

Leadership implications in the context of rising proportion of work that will be done in various hybrid formats are multi-fold. First, post-heroic leaders need to fight the always-on culture and in general help creating healthy organizations. Second, post-heroic leaders along with their teams and organizations need to co-define boundaries between work and private life, even though they are physically blurred. Third, post-heroic leaders need to place emphasis on psychological safety and justice between the core and the periphery of their organization, between those who work in the office and are close to the information and to the resource flow and those far from it. Different needs of both groups need to be communicated and dealt with. Edmondson and Mortensen (2021) argue that psychological safety is one of the strongest predictors of team effectiveness and that without it, the hybrid work will not work. Post-heroic leadership in its core is therefore well-suited to create psychological safety in hybrid environments.

3.2 Algorithmic Management vs. Humanizing Hybrid Work

The rise of hybrid work is opening up the space for another important and fundamental consideration of how leaders should approach their profession. The fact is that more people will spend more time off the traditional company premises. Does that call for tighter control enabled with omnipresent technological advances? Or do we need to resort to trust, autonomy, and mastery? In other words, do leaders in hybrid work need to exercise algorithmic management, or is it time for a renaissance of humanizing management? The situation again calls for post-heroic leadership, and I would like to provide some more justification for it. To do so, we will take a short trip through the history of management thought.

Scientific management (Taylor, 1903, 1911, 1926) is a movement beginning in the end of the nineteenth century, which introduced the principle of in-depth understanding and optimization of work processes into modern production. In the last two decades of the nineteenth century, the idea grew into a movement that, thanks to its most vocal advocate, Frederick Winslow Taylor, gained widespread recognition and a well-established title: Taylorism. In the beginning of the twentieth century, the movement experienced growth, and, from its initial four principles, became known mainly for its ultimate focus on maximizing work efficiency and strict control of managers over the work of employees and the processes they deal with.

The ultimate example was the so-called therbligs (Meredith, 1953) of the Gilbreths, who were engaged in microstudies of movements. Their goal was to break down the work to the smallest possible tasks and each task to the smallest possible movement. When they then broke even such a small task into 12 therbligs, after careful analysis, they found that three of them could actually be omitted. By doing so, however, they completely dehumanized work and forgot about everything that makes people humans, not machines. It is not surprising that the period of "scientific" management and criticism (Price, 2003) that it is false, a pseudoscience, was followed by a period of humanization of business, which returned focus on people back into business. Humanistic management (Melé, 2016; Spitzeck, 2011) puts human well-being and dignity (Pirson, 2017) into the forefront as a counterbalance to the dehumanization to which Taylorism has led in its extreme form.

History likes to repeat itself and the COVID-19 pandemic is revealing this in the most apparent way. Many organizations found themselves quite unprepared for a situation where the organization is suddenly no longer a group of more or less collocated individuals coordinating their activities to achieve common goals. Even after the pandemic is mastered, and as we are transitioning to more hybrid forms of work, the challenge for most leaders is to keep together people who do at least an important part of their work remotely.

At least two diametrically opposed solutions are offered, which can be roughly summarized in a group of algorithmic management or humanization of business, control, or trust. For a long time now, there has been an increase in the so-called algorithmic management, which is projected in various forms. Some call it uberization (Möhlmann & Zalmanson, 2017), others new public management (Veale & Brass, 2019), and some simply call it micromanagement.

In short, close monitoring and directing the behaviour of members of organizations, measuring everything, everyone, and everywhere. To top it all off, we add a pinch of artificial intelligence, gamification, and promoting unhealthy competition among employees. An important share of major technological companies is more or less openly flirting with such solutions and often even praise them and offer them to all of us as a form of salvation. The only problem is that these systems are a bigger part of the problem than of the solution.

Micromanagement, backed by surveillance technologies, can really squeeze the best out of a person, while at the same time it can bring out the worst in us. In the psychology of organizational and educational environments, we speak of the so-called Golem effect (Veale & Brass, 2019). Lower expectations of organizations spirally lead members to even worse results.

We argue that hybrid work requires even more humanizing at work and therefore calls for even more of post-heroic leadership in action. Investing into the resilience of people and organizations, strengthening healthy relationships, preventing toxic cultures, training managers to work in changing conditions, fostering innovation; all of these are major themes of today's business world and determinants of business success.

Recently, Hamel and Zannini (2020) criticized the prevailing bureaucratic model of organizations, which stifles creativity, innovation, adaptability, and resilience of organizations. They offer an overview of the latest research in the field of humanization of work as well as practical examples and tools for developing humanistic organizations. Their message could not have come at a more relevant moment with the rise of hybrid work. So, what is it that holds together people who are not in the same place at the same time?

Plethora of recent research is united in at least two elements—trust and meaning. We need to know why we are there and understand the contribution of our work. When we earn trust, there is no stronger binder. Both meaning and trust trigger a psychological mechanism called the Pygmalion effect (Eden, 1990). High expectations lead to even higher results. In this case, it is a spiral upwards. The humanization of business is striking back, and post-heroic leadership is at the forefront and looking ahead. Leading people in hybrid work needs to be even more servant and shared, therefore, post-heroic.

References

Aleksić, D., & Černe, M. (2020). *Ko prožno delo postane nuja*. HR&M.

Aleksić, D., Černe, M., & Sajevec, L. (2020). *Kako dolgo lahko zaposleni "zmrzujemo" na daljavo?* CPOEF E-TALK. School of Economics and Business, UL.

Bailenson, J. N. (2021). Nonverbal overload: A theoretical argument for the causes of zoom fatigue. *Technology, Mind, and Behavior, 2*(1).

Choudhury, P. R. (2020, November–December). Our work-from-anywhere future. *Harvard Business Review*.

Dingel, J., & Neiman, B. (2020). How many jobs can be done at home? *Journal of Public Economics, 189*, 104235.

Eden, D. (1990). *Pygmalion in management: Productivity as a self-fulfilling prophecy*. Lexington Books/D. C. Heath and Com.

Edmondson, A. C., & Mortensen, M. (2021). What psychological safety looks like in a hybrid workplace. *Harvard Business Review*.

Fayard, A.-L., Weeks, J., & Khan, M. (2021, March–April). Designing the hybrid office. *Harvard Business Review*.

Fossilien, L., & Duff, M. W. (2020). How to combat zoom fatigue? *Harvard Business Review*, p. 29.

Gartner. (2020). *Gartner HR survey reveals 41% of employees likely to work remotely at least some of the time post coronavirus pandemic* [Press release]. https://www.gartner.com/en/newsroom/press-releases/2020-04-14-gartner-hr-survey-reveals-41--of-employees-likely-to-

Gratton, L. (2021, May–June). How to do hybrid right. *Harvard Business Review*.

Halford, S. (2005). Hybrid workspace: Re-spatialisations of work, organisation and management. *New Technology, Work and Employment*, 20.

Hamel, G., & Zanini, M. (2020). *Humanocracy: Creating organizations as amazing as the people inside them*. Harvard Business Press.

Kniffin, K. M., Narayanan, J., Anseel, F., Antonakis, J., Ashford, S. P., Bakker, A. B., Bamberger, P., Bapuji, H., Bhave, D. P., Choi, V. K., Creary, S. J., Demerouti, E., Flynn, F. J., Gelfand, M. J., Greer, L. L., Johns, G., Kesebir, S., Klein, P. G., Lee, S. Y., ... Vugt, M. v. (2021). COVID-19 and the workplace: Implications, issues, and insights for future research and action. *American Psychologist, 76*(1), 63–77.

Melé, D. (2016). Understanding Humanistic Management. *Humanistic Management Journal, 1*(1), 33–55.

Meredith, G. P. (1953). Theory of the "Therblig." *Occupational Psychology, 27*, 128–136.

Morris, B. (2020). Why does zoom exhaust you? Science has an answer. *The Wall Street Journal*. https://www.wsj.com/articles/why-does-zoom-exhaust-you-science-has-an-answer-11590600269

Möhlmann, M., & Zalmanson, L. (2017). *Hands on the wheel: Navigating algorithmic management and Uber drivers' autonomy*.

Petriglieri, G., Ashford, S. J., & Wrzesniewski, A. (2018). Agony and ecstasy in the gig economy: Cultivating holding environments for precarious and personalized work identities. *Administrative Science Quarterly, 64*(1), 124–170.

Pirson, M. (2017). *Humanistic management: Protecting dignity and promoting well-being*. Cambridge University Press.

Price, M. P. (2003). Frank and Lillian Gilbreth and the motion study controversy, 1907–1930. In J. C. Wood & M. C. Wood (Eds.), *Frank and Lillian Gilbreth: Critical evaluations in business and management* (Vol. 2, pp. 455). Routledge.

Spataro, J. (2020). *The future of work—The good, the challenging & the unknown*. https://www.microsoft.com/en-us/microsoft-365/blog/2020/07/08/future-work-good-challenging-unknown/

Spitzeck, H. (2011). An integrated model of humanistic management. *Journal of Business Ethics, 99*(1), 51–62.

Taylor, F. W. (1903). *Shop management*. American Society of Mechanical Engineers.

Taylor, F. W. (1911). *The principles of scientific management*. Harper & Brothers.

Taylor, F. W. (1926). *Taylor's testimony Before the Special House Committee*. Taylor Society.

Veale, M., & Brass, I. (2019). *Administration by algorithm?* Public management meets Public Sector Machine Learning.

Woldoff, R. A., & Litchfield, R. C. (2021). *Digital nomads: In search of freedom, community, and meaningful work in the new economy*. Oxford University Press.

PART II

Process of Post-Heroic Leadership

Times call for better ways how we can think and enact leadership in societies, organizations, and teams alike. Part I of this monograph highlighted the context and reasons why we need post-heroic leadership in the first place. The leadership that is both shared and servant in its nature. Readers can also benefit from ample qualitative data demonstrating post-heroic leadership in the series of acts and experience of experts becoming leaders. Furthermore, readers were able to delve deeper into the context of hybrid work and into the particular role of postheroic leadership under such circumstances.

In Part II, we will examine the process and manifestations of post-heroic leadership. Post-heroic leadership is a kind of leadership that combines elements of servant and shared leadership. We aim to examine in more depth, how do we see post-heroic leadership manifests itself in action and how does it unfold.

Chapter 4 explores how does an expert become a post-heroic leader. The act or better said a process of becoming a leader is a complex and decisive in formation of leadership styles and patterns. It is a gear-shifting situation and often experienced, in which many of the underlying, implicit theories about leadership, followership, and people in general materialize. Therefore, I dedicate a special chapter to it.

Chapter 5 is bestowed to somehow overlooked dimension of sustainable development goals—sustainable workplace. I argue (and demonstrate with qualitative data) that post-heroic leadership can help develop workplaces that are sustainable both for employees and for leaders themselves.

Chapter 6 revolves around the myths and science of successful leadership of change. Engaging and involving styles and behaviours are those that have the capacity of adequately addressing change both at psychological as well as organizational level.

Chapter 7 addresses another vital part of the post-heroic leadership process—creating community and building collaborative culture. The narratives and qualitative data we gathered show that shared cultures are built through servant and humble leadership behaviours.

CHAPTER 4

Becoming a Post-Heroic Leader: From Expert to Leader

Abstract Becoming a leader often means transitioning from the field of expertise into the field of the (relative) unknown. Just like being an expert, leadership is a profession requiring constant competence development. Organizations aiming to choose and develop post-heroic leaders focus on (1) choosing the right people for the job, (2) developing dimensions of servant leadership: humility, empowerment, authenticity, interpersonal acceptance, providing direction, and stewardship; and (3) encouraging sharedness: social support, voice, and shared purpose. Followers' implicit leadership theories need to change from heroic towards post-heroic.

Keywords Expert · Leader · Follower · Change leadership · Expert leadership · Leadership competencies

4.1 Transitioning from an Expert to a Leader

In numerous professional organizations, such as hospitals, universities, and other knowledge-intensive organizations, it is rather frequent that a career path of a leader stems from a promotion of a top expert to a leadership position in an organization. It is also rather frequent for newly appointed leaders who used to be at the top of their game as experts to

M. Škerlavaj, *Post-Heroic Leadership*,
https://doi.org/10.1007/978-3-030-90820-1_4

realise that leadership is also a profession. Soon newly appointed leaders tend to realise that they have not been properly prepared for such a demanding profession. Let us have a look at a couple of reflections about expert transitions to leadership roles.

Damjan Osredkar, neuropediatrician, renowned researcher with a global track record, medical doctor, and the head of the Clinical Department of Child, Adolescent and Developmental Neurology at the Paediatric clinic of the University Medical Centre Ljubljana reflects on his transition from a top-notch expert to a brand-new leader:

> In the beginning, the change was significant. I really loved doing my job and then suddenly, I found myself in a situation where I was completely lost … (Hlača Ferjančič et al., 2019)

Newly appointed leaders also learn that their new role effects relations with former colleagues:

> The first thing I felt was that I became completely alone, not because my colleagues would avoid me, but simply because I had to find my new place and to distance myself from what I have been doing before. (Hlača Ferjančič et al., 2019)

4.2 Choosing the Right People for the Job

Why do experts want to be leaders in the first place? Well, often they do not. Still, in professional and knowledge-intensive organizations, having sufficient domain-specific knowledge (Goodall, 2012) is both a prerequisite and a source of credibility and reference power to be accepted as a leader among colleagues (Stoller et al., 2016).

To understand how an organization works, leaders need domain-specific knowledge. Therefore, to really understand some professional organizations in industries such as health care, education, information technology, media, and so on, leaders need to understand their context and specifics. Thus, there is no doubt that an expert is better positioned for leadership. At the same time, this is another opportunity for all of us to recognize leadership as a profession. Relying merely on feelings, intuition, what we observe and mimic is not enough. However, there is evidence to show that a minor part of experts actually wants to become leaders (Goodall & Bäker, 2015). Or that they become one for the wrong kind of reasons.

How should we then select the right leaders for the job and not be tricked by over-confidence in place of leadership competence? Especially when all they have is leadership potential rather than a proven track record. I suggest starting with finding people with the right kind of motivations, and the motivation should be to serve a common good rather than own ego or power needs. There is an ongoing debate whether power reveals or corrupts (Grant, 2019, Decelles et al., 2012). There is ample evidence of the dark tetrad psychological states being overly represented at the top of organizations compared to the general populations (Furnham et al., 2013). Recruitment and selection are generally demanding and decisive human resource management processes, and they are even more important in the context of leadership. The impact of leadership might be indirect, but it has a multiplying effect on the work and life of numerous people.

Osredkar (Hlača Ferjančič et al., 2019) reflects on his motivation for accepting the leadership role:

> I took over the department at a very turbulent time. There were two groups of people who didn't understand each other very well, which led to quite a lot of conflict. Sometimes it happens that you are plunged into it [leadership role] or you decide to do it yourself because you think that somehow you could help. In our case, however, we have managed to overcome these conflicts, and, in fact, we now understand each other much better and work well together. We shifted our focus from our personal issues to medical issues.

4.3 Developing Post-Heroic Leadership Competencies

How can organizations help new leaders develop post-heroic leadership competencies? There is an evident need for it.

> I think it would be very helpful for me if I had some formal knowledge or if I went through some schooling where I could adapt to this [new leadership role] and maybe I wouldn't lose so much energy later, by learning along the way. (Osredkar in Hlača Ferjančič et al., 2019)

In the absence of proper leadership development, some of the newly appointed leaders resort to mimicking behaviours, social learning, and social contagion. This is how poor practices of leadership spread like wildfire. There is an anecdote from the elementary school setting, where a new leader required his former, long-standing colleagues to use an official form of address for him as he moved into the new role. Naturally, this awkward attempt to establish distance was accepted with a fair amount of ridicule. Osredkar observes (Hlača Ferjančič et al., 2019):

> I still see people here who come to a leadership position and then can't help to constantly prove how important they are and what they can do. Sometimes they even do themselves harm by doing so, because they are somehow making fun of themselves. It is clear to everyone else that they are doing this out of some inner need and that this way of working is not very effective.

Instead, demonstrating some of the post-heroic leadership dimensions would be in place (Lehman et al., 2019; Newman, 2019) empowerment and development are the first dimensions of servant leadership, one of two-integral first order constructs of post-heroic leadership. Osredkar reflects upon his decision to assume an empowering and developmental style of servant leadership:

> We have twelve departments at the paediatric clinic. Each department has its own way of managing and I don't know which management style is actually the best. I chose the one where the hierarchical structure is much less pronounced than it was in its most prominent time. Then it was very clear where the professors were sitting, where the specialists were and where the students were, and it was almost a sin not to abide by something like that. Therefore, I have a very equal relationship with my co-workers. Basically, you don't need to run the place with a heavy hand to get things moving in the right direction. (Hlača Ferjančič et al., 2019)

Grega Milčinski is another post-heroic leader who grew from an expert to a founder of a high-tech company Sinergise which partners with top global companies. When interviewed about leadership practices at their company, he also talks about empowerment and trust:

> People in our company have a great deal of autonomy. I think the most important thing is that we trust them, I regard this as crucial. We trust a

> person from the first day they come into the company, and they have our trust until they do something to lose it. This trust is reflected in giving them very responsible tasks very quickly. I think that is the main freedom that people have. (Hlača Ferjančič et al., 2019)

In terms of interpersonal acceptance, Osredkar (in Hlača Ferjančič et al., 2019) narrates about his formative experience as an expert and reflects upon his leadership models:

> When I worked in Oslo or San Francisco, I realized that the world's most masterful medical professionals have always been such wonderful, simple, warm people who didn't try to tear everything from the hands of everyone else just because they could. They were simply the exact opposite—the ones who gave the most of themselves. These were one of my first mentors who gave me assignments that seemed very big to me because I, at the time, thought I was incapable of doing them. One also grows a lot through it.

At face value, providing direction in shared and servant leadership might seem challenging. The interview data we gathered proves the contrary. When multidisciplinary teams are involved in setting direction for complex tasks, the results are better. A shared purpose is established. Some organizations go as far as "unbossing" their cultures and replacing them with shared direction setting. Milčinski comments:

> I would expect for them [potential leaders] to be multifunctional, as my work assignments appear in many different areas and problems occur in many different places. People are obsessed with »managing«, they have »tasks« and keep all things very tidy. This works very well on paper, but in practice it transforms a person who is a very capable intellectual into someone who works behind a conveyor belt. It kills half of their energy, half of their intellect, and all just because you want them to work exactly like you do. In principle, the people we employ are better than I am.
>
> So, why would I be telling them how to work? It does not make sense. And still, this is often done because there is no trust between people. It seems to me that everyone looks at employees as if they are going to try to take advantage of a situation, steal things, work as little as possible and do as little as possible. This is not the case in practice. If you put people in an organized work environment, it seems to me that people will be happy to contribute. After all, they have to spend those eight hours there, and people want to do something useful. (Hlača Ferjančič et al., 2019)

Humility and stewardship are another two crucial competencies of post-heroic leadership, reflected in the following statement:

> I'm not some kind of a leadership expert, I'm still a self-taught leader and I think I'll remain so until the end. Personally, I tackle this by talking a lot with my colleagues at regular meetings or in one-on-one meetings. Collectively, we try to identify problems and we also look for solutions. As a department, we adopted a lot of solutions that were not my own. They were pointed out by my colleagues who have even more experience in certain areas, or who noticed something better, expressed it, and I personally thought it was a very good idea, so we made the change. (Osredkar in Hlača Ferjančič, et al., 2019)

4.4 Changing Followers' Implicit Leadership Theories

The second, equally if not even more, important question is how to prepare followers to change their predominant expectations about their leaders. In other words, how can we steer followers' implicit leadership theories (Eden & Leviatan, 1975; Foti et al., 2017) away from so deeply rooted autocratic patterns towards post-heroic leadership expectations. After all, leadership is a relational phenomenon that does not exist without followers' legitimacy (Dutton & Spreitzer, 2014; Fairhurst & Antonakis, 2012; Uhl-Bien, 2011). Therefore, followers need to be engaged in the change process of altering awareness and expectations on what actually works in leadership. There is illusion that predominant patterns still converge towards leader-centred focus. An important explanation can be found in our bias to mix up over-confidence with competence (Ronay et al., 2019).

I argue that one possible way of improving follower implicit leadership theories is by inviting followers to contribute to the task at hand and by creating a sense of sharedness. Shared leadership (D'Innocenzo et al., 2014; Wang et al., 2013; Wu et al., 2018), as one of two central first order constructs of post-heroic leadership, is demonstrated by creating a shared purpose, providing social support, and inviting voice (Carson et al., 2007). Osredkar reports on example of a change he initiated by creating the sense of sharedness:

> Recently, we completely reorganized an entire department, which was a big change in the organization, in the work between doctors and nurses, and in the way the patients are received. In short, a lot of perturbations. Quite a few people were not in favour of these changes because it is easier for them if everything runs on autopilot. In the end, it seems to me that we will move to a state that will be better for everyone; better for the patients and for our work, and most likely some time will be left for us to strengthen the research side of our work and write about what we have learned along the way. (Hlača Ferjančič et al., 2019)

Furthermore, Osredkar also reflects on gaining legitimacy as a leader in a hospital setting:

> Basically, we were learning all the time. All I asked my colleagues in the beginning was to give me a chance, because I didn't have any assurances that they could trust, I didn't have any real leadership experience. In the past, I led a small group in Oslo, I gained a bit of experience in some other circumstances, but basically, I didn't have any clear leadership skills that would be obvious and provable to everyone. I was pretty lost at first and my colleagues were also very careful around me. I think things started to fall into place along the way with each successful step. The first steps were initially small and the ones that were very necessary; the ones where it was obvious to everyone that they needed to be done.
>
> We have completely reorganized the work for patients with neuromuscular diseases. Although this was again a major change, in the end it proved to be a very successful intervention. We are now invited to lecture in countries across Europe and are cited as an example of successful change for the better. (Osredkar in Hlača Ferjančič, et al., 2019)

Similarly, Milčinski reflects upon the shared purpose and meaning making as a key motivational driver:

> … after all, people work for half the time they are awake. They put a lot of energy into work, and it is crucial that they know they're doing something meaningful and that they themselves have an impact on what they do. (Milčinski in Hlača Ferjančič et al., 2019)

Post-heroic leaders are quite aware that an alternative route, one of micromanaging is doomed to fail:

I knew from the very beginning that I could not do everything by myself. But I also knew that if I had such an appetite to be in charge of everything in all areas, I would be doomed to fail. So, one of the first things we did was that we divided the areas very carefully and that each of these areas has its own leader now. (Osredkar in Hlača Ferjančič et al., 2019)

References

Beck, R. J., & Harter, J. (n.d.). *Why great managers are so rare*. https://www.gallup.com/workplace/231593/why-great-managers-rare.aspx

Carson, J., Tesluk, P., & Marrone, J. (2007). Shared leadership in teams: An investigation of antecedent conditions and performance. *Academy of Management Journal, 50*, 1217–1234.

Decelles, K., DeRue, D., Margolis, J., & Ceranic, T. (2012). Does power corrupt or enable? When and why power facilitates self-interested behavior. *The Journal of Applied Psychology, 97*, 681–689.

Dutton, J. E., & Spreitzer, G. M. (2014). *How to be a positive leader: Small actions, big impact*. Berrett-Koehler Publishers.

D'Innocenzo, L., Mathieu, J. E., & Kukenberger, M. R. (2014). A meta-analysis of different forms of shared leadership-team performance relations. *Journal of Management, 42*(7), 1964–1991.

Eden, D., & Leviatan, U. (1975). Implicit leadership theory as a determinant of the factor structure underlying supervisory behavior scales. *Journal of Applied Psychology, 60*(6), 736–741.

Fairhurst, G., & Antonakis, J. (2012). A research agenda for relational leadership (pp. 433–459). Information Age Publishing.

Foti, R. J., Hansbrough, T. K., Epitropaki, O., & Coyle, P. T. (2017). Dynamic viewpoints on implicit leadership and followership theories: Approaches, findings, and future directions. *The Leadership Quarterly, 28*(2), 261–267.

Furnham, A., Richards, S. C., & Paulhus, D. L. (2013). The dark triad of personality: A 10 year review. *Social and Personality Psychology Compass, 7*(3), 199–216.

Goodall, A., & Bäker, A. (2015). A theory exploring how expert leaders influence performance in knowledge-intensive organizations (pp. 49–68). In *Incentives and performance*. Springer.

Goodall, A. H. (2012). A theory of expert leaders. *Academy of Management Proceedings, 2012*(1), 14411.

Grant, A. (2019). *Power doesn't corrupt. It just exposes who leaders really are*. https://www.washingtonpost.com/business/economy/power-doesnt-corrupt-it-just-exposes-who-leaders-really-are/2019/02/22/f5680116-3600-11e9-854a-7a14d7fec96a_story.html

Hlača Ferjančič et al. (2019a). *Vodenje s posluhom 1/5: od eksperta do vodje.* https://val202.rtvslo.si/2019/12/poslovno-gospodarske-teme-16/

Lehman, D. W., O'Connor, K., & Carroll, G. R. (2019). Acting on authenticity: Individual interpretations and behavioral responses. *Review of General Psychology, 23*(1), 19–31.

Newman, G. E. (2019). The psychology of authenticity. *Review of General Psychology, 23*(1), 8–18.

Ronay, R., Oostrom, J. K., Lehmann-Willenbrock, N., Mayoral, S., & Rusch, H. (2019). Playing the trump card: Why we select overconfident leaders and why it matters. *The Leadership Quarterly, 30*(6), 101316.

Stoller, J. K., Goodall, A., & Baker, A. (2016). Why the best hospitals are managed by doctors. *Harvard Business Review*. https://hbr.org/2016/12/why-the-best-hospitals-are-managed-by-doctors

Uhl-Bien, M. (2011). Relational leadership theory: Exploring the social processes of leadership and organizing. In P. Werhane & M. Painter-Morland (Eds.), *Leadership, gender, and organization. Issues in business ethics* (Vol. 27). Springer.

Wang, D., Waldman, D., & Zhang, Z. (2013). A meta-analysis of shared leadership and team effectiveness. *The Journal of Applied Psychology, 99.*

Wu, Q., Cormican, K., & Chen, G. (2018). A meta-analysis of shared leadership: Antecedents, consequences, and moderators. *Journal of Leadership & Organizational Studies, 27*, 49–64.

CHAPTER 5

Sustainable Post-Heroic Leadership Practices

Abstract From the organizational point of view, sustainable development goals do not put enough emphasis on sustainability in the workplace. Post-heroic leadership practices can help make leadership more sustainable. Their use can ensure employee well-being and prevent over-exploitation of human resources. Inadequate leadership practices can pose a major risk for well-being of both leaders and followers. The importance of stakeholders is discussed, for both leaders and followers. The resilience of a leader is built in cooperation with other team members, and they should exercise servant and shared leadership behaviours and ensure psychological safety of their followers.

Keywords Sustainable leadership · Employee well-being · Well-doing · Resilience · Sustainable development goals

5.1 Post-Heroic Leadership—The Missing Piece of the Sustainability Puzzle

Sustainability became a mainstream societal and research topic over years. As environmental challenges are mounting, UN Sustainable Development Goals (United Nations, 2015) present an adequate conceptual framework in addressing them at the international and national policy level as

M. Škerlavaj, *Post-Heroic Leadership*,
https://doi.org/10.1007/978-3-030-90820-1_5

they provide direction and measurement tools for countries to compare themselves to each other (Schmidt-Traub et al., 2017). Their purpose is to tackle multiple challenges humankind is facing to ensure well-being, economic prosperity, and environmental protection (Pradhan et al., 2017). At the same time, there is an increasing awareness that focusing on macro-levels and sustainability reporting will not create actual impact (Pucker, 2021).

We do not emphasize the vital dimension of sustainability at work enough, despite some recent efforts to incorporate sustainability in leadership development (Peterlin, 2016). There is much more we need to learn, study, and practice in how do deal with people in organizations in a sustainable way. This chapter will focus on the idea that healthy, post-heroic leadership is the one that does not overexploit key organizational resource—people and their health. We argue that sustainable leadership needs to be sustainable for employees, their leaders, and organizations as a whole to balance well-being with well-doing (Huppert et al., 2005; Peccei & Voorde, 2019; Wright & Cropanzano, 2000). I will also provide qualitative data from organizations exercising sustainable post-heroic leadership.

5.2 How to Make Organizational Life Sustainable for Followers?

Previous research demonstrates strong relationship among various leadership behaviours and employee well-being (Arnold et al., 2007; Inceoglu et al., 2018; Kuoppala et al., 2008; van Dierendonck et al., 2004). Meta-analytical evidence (Kuoppala et al., 2008) shows that inadequate leadership turns out to be a major risk factor for reduction in employee well-being. Leadership is part of the problem. We would like to examine whether it can also be part of the solution. Gathered qualitative data is showing that different elements of post-heroic leadership can help create a more sustainable organizational life for followers.

Mikro+Polo, the largest Slovenian laboratory supplier, is an organization well-known for its sustainable leadership and human resource management practices. Aleksandra Peharda (Hlača Ferjančič et al., 2019), director of the laboratory programme, comments on unlimited paid annual leave they are offering to their employees:

> This is just one of the goodies the company is offering. We take care of a good atmosphere and a positive climate. We also allow our employees to bring their pets to our premises. We enable them to optimally combine private life and work.

Given the complete autonomy to take paid time off their work, employees reciprocate with responsibility:

> It is interesting to see that the number of vacation days has not changed significantly. This freedom gives autonomy to the individual, or the possibility of growth. Young people may take a day, two more of vacation, or even 5 days, because they like to travel. Our employees take from 25 to 35 days off, but they always make sure the work is done because they feel responsible. That is why I say that responsibility is actually a privilege that we emphasize very much in our company. (Hlača Ferjančič et al., 2019)

The signal of trust the Mikro+Polo is giving as an organization and as their leaders, is more important than the number of vacation days itself. The message of such post-heroic leadership is that employees are responsible human beings, worthy of our trust, and have the autonomy to decide how they will contribute to this organization. The opposite situation is if you give people a "budget" and you say: "you can only spend this much". What happens then, of course, is that people spend precisely to the last cent.

Another important consideration is related to those instances when trust is broken. How should post-heroic leaders behave in such circumstances? Aleksandra Peharda comments on situations when trust was broken:

> That also happens, of course. It is not ideal, not a fairy tale. Doing business is not a fairy tale either. We face many challenges, and thank goodness we have a strong team, support, where we debate a lot about the situations that have arisen. It is interesting, however, that people usually find out for themselves that something is wrong and also on their own initiative speak about these mistakes, reasons for them and justifications, and not only that, but they also propose an idea of how to fix it, so that certain things would not happen again in the future. Being able to make mistakes is ultimately a privilege again. Others who are unable to internalize this, however, do not feel good in our company. (Hlača Ferjančič et al., 2019)

Similarly, at Mikro+Polo, they extend their efforts for sustainable and responsible behaviour towards their community and work along with social enterprises to distribute all the remaining food from their canteen each day at 1 p.m. to deprivileged members of their local community.

The above-illustrated case is an example of stakeholderism (Atkinson et al., 1997) in action. An idea that company does not exist for the mere interest of shareholders (profit), but that is also has other important stakeholders with their respective goals that the company should simultaneously attend to. It is very interesting to observe the twists and turns in the very concept of the purpose of the company's existence. After decades of shareholderism prevailing, there is an increasing awareness that companies exist not only because of their owners, but that they also exist because of other stakeholders. Since the 1970s, it has been widely known in Europe, that stakeholder theory is what sustainable organizations should follow and that it is not just owners' theory that is important. The concept of sustainable leadership is quite broad, but it is basically about treating people in a respectful, supportable, and sustainable way. In such a context, practising post-heroic leadership has a strong potential for sustainable use of human resources in organizations.

Mikro+Polo is also a case to show how post-heroic leadership is demonstrating the positive impact on sustainable business and its bottom line:

> Relaxed people, people who are happy, give significantly more. Only after that can we say that we are creating greater added value. Of course, in the end, every business brags about its success, validation, and money that allows it to afford all of this. If we internalize a lot of soft skills as a company culture, it comes for free. If people also sincerely believe in it, then all of this is very simple. Even when there is a crisis. There was a crisis also in our company and people lost their jobs. Nevertheless, we stayed together, got together and discussed about what to do and how to do it, where we are going. This is one point where passing information from management seems very important to me. Management, of course, sets the culture and everything else, and after that, it is extremely important to deliver this information directly to all of us employees. (Hlača Ferjančič et al., 2019)

5.3 How to Make Post-Heroic Leadership Sustainable for Leaders?

In order for post-heroic leadership to work, it has to be sustainable also for those who exercise it. During times of change, many leaders reported and some of us also experienced, the increasing demand of leader's time and other resources (Demerouti et al., 2017). To keep the strings together, when organizational members are apart, takes special care and attention. Therefore, a growing research interest in the concept and interventions (Gray & Jones, 2018; Panaccio et al., 2015; Quirk et al., 2018; Roche & Haar, 2013; Urrila, 2021) aimed at improving well-being of leaders comes as no surprise.

In conversation with Tomaž Lanišek (Hlača Ferjančič et al., 2020), we examined ways for organizations to build sustainable ways of work for post-heroic leaders themselves. Lanišek is the head of smart city project at the City Municipality of Kranj, and former top manager with experience from a variety of sectors, including manufacturing. Upon completing his mandate as a CEO of Knauf Insulation in Slovenia, he took a sabbatical to strengthen his resilience. He spent the year at one of the most prestigious business schools to replenish his resources. Reflecting on the year, he talks about other ways of replenishing a leader's depleted resources:

> I really like to travel around Slovenia and to other countries as a photographer. This year, I travelled around my close surroundings, and I must say that our country really is beautiful, and I could join both the pleasant and the useful. (Hlača Ferjančič et al., 2020)

In the era and region where most of adult human identity revolves around the work we do and where hard work is a norm, even taking vacations can be a point of consideration. On that note, Lanišek reflects:

> It is important to disconnect, to not think about the daily business. There is no need to wait for a holiday, but it is necessary to work on its daily variant; the afternoons or evenings must be private. However, I have always been a supporter of people being on leave for two weeks at a time, which is also a legal requirement, and it makes sense that it is a legal requirement, so that people really disconnect and then come back with new ideas, rested, with new enthusiasm and motivation. So that is crucial, even if you have a job that makes you so happy that you don't even know that you are going to work. Even if you always enjoy it so much, it can always be a challenge

> if you get to the point of oversaturation and it is better to go on vacation sooner than to get to that point or beyond. (Hlača Ferjančič et al., 2020)

In fact, something that can possibly lead us to be promoted to the level of a leader is also a risk factor for burnout. Research (Lee & Ashforth, 1996; Swider & Zimmerman, 2010) in personality traits shows that conscientiousness helps in career development and success, even for leaders. However, in combination with agreeableness, it is also significantly related to the risk of burnout via emotional exhaustion in particular. Then there is a rise in job demands posed by always on culture (McDowall & Kinman, 2017) and anywhere-anytime business models of hybrid work that increase the risk of reduced well-being at work (Conway et al., 2015). It is harmful for the health of individuals, and the organization does not actually benefit from it.

Lanišek recalls his time as the CEO at Knauf Insulation and is convinced that a leader can strengthen his resilience with an empowered team around them:

> The team is the key. I have always emphasized its importance. If the team works well, then it is easier to survive. The worst thing is if you have to do certain things yourself that others would be able do. When you build a team, you have to find people who are motivated, and who know more about their field of work than you. And then you have to let them do the work. Because if you think you are the smartest, then everything will be the way you decide for yourself, however, then you also have to do most of the work yourself. (Hlača Ferjančič et al., 2020)

His point is also that a sustainable leadership as well as followership is characterized by psychological safety, in alignment with ample research evidence by Edmondson and his colleagues (A. Edmondson & Lei, 2014; A. C. Edmondson, 2018):

> We had and still have a system in Knauf Insulation, where mistakes are allowed, but are not to be repeated, and lessons can be learned from them. Because every one of us makes mistakes, but only in this way can you innovate and make progress. And when people get this feeling that there is not any kind of punishment if something goes wrong, then they embrace their role and do the job. That is that key part, and then of course let people be free and serve them as much as possible, because each of us has a different motivation. (Hlača Ferjančič et al., 2020)

The conceptual answer to the initially posed question about the sustainable approaches towards post-heroic leadership therefore lies in the ways how leaders exercise servant behaviours. Grant's (2013) learnings still apply—post-heroic leaders need to act in an otherish manner in order for their colleagues, themselves, and their organizations as a whole to flourish and prosper. To exercise servant and shared leadership in a manner that is sustainable both for them and for their colleagues. Ms. Peharda comments on leader's open door and quiet-hours policy:

> The leader must also do their job. I have been dealing with this for a long time. I like open doors, but these are simply distractions. Whichever way you look at it, every person entering your office is a distraction. So, I imposed a quiet rule that by 8 a.m. no one should enter my office. I am most productive at that time; I do what is necessary and I must be concentrated. I have to say we stick to that. (Hlača Ferjančič et al., 2019)

While there are numerous leadership practices available to exercise sustainable leadership, it should be duly noted that sustainable leadership is taking proper care of both employees and leaders.

References

Arnold, K., Turner, N., Barling, J., Kelloway, K., & McKee, M. (2007). Transformational leadership and psychological well-being: The mediating role of meaningful work. *Journal of Occupational Health Psychology, 12*, 193–203.

Atkinson, A. A., Waterhouse, J. H., & Wells, R. B. (1997). A stakeholder approach to strategic performance measurement. *MIT Sloan Management Review, 38*(3), 25.

Conway, E., Fu, N., Monks, K., Alfes, K., & Bailey, C. (2015). Demands or resources? The relationship between HR practices, employee engagement, and emotional exhaustion within a hybrid model of employment relations. *Human Resource Management, 55*(5), 901–917.

Demerouti, E., Heuvel, M., Xanthopoulou, D., Dubbelt, L., & Gordon, H. (2017). Job resources as contributors to wellbeing. In C. L. Cooper & M. P. Leiter (Eds.), *The Routledge companion to wellbeing at work* (pp. 269–283). Routledge.

Edmondson, A., & Lei, Z. (2014). Psychological safety: The history, renaissance, and future of an interpersonal construct. *Annual Review of Organizational Psychology and Organizational Behavior, 1*, 23–43.

Edmondson, A. C. (2018). *The fearless organization: Creating psychological safety in the workplace for learning, innovation, and growth*. Wiley.

Grant, A. M. (2013). *Give and take: A revolutionary approach to success*. Penguin.
Gray, D., & Jones, K. (2018). The resilience and wellbeing of public sector leaders. *International Journal of Public Leadership, 14*(3), 138–154.
Hlača Ferjančič et al. (2019). *Vodenje s posluhom 2/5: Naj traja - dopust ali motivacija?* https://val202.rtvslo.si/2020/01/poslovno-gospodarske-teme-17/
Hlača Ferjančič et al. (2020). *Vodenje s posluhom: Krepitev odpornosti vodij*. https://val202.rtvslo.si/2020/09/poslovno-gospodarske-teme-41/
Huppert, F. A., Baylis, N., & Keverne, B. (2005). *The science of well-being*. Oxford University Press.
Inceoglu, I., Thomas, G., Chu, C., Plans, D., & Gerbasi, A. (2018). Leadership behavior and employee well-being: An integrated review and a future research agenda. *The Leadership Quarterly, 29*(1), 179–202.
Kuoppala, J., Lamminpää, A., Liira, J., & Vainio, H. (2008). Leadership, job well-being, and health effects—A systematic review and a meta-analysis. *Journal of Occupational and Environmental Medicine/American College of Occupational and Environmental Medicine, 50*, 904–915.
Lee, R. T., & Ashforth, B. E. (1996). A meta-analytic examination of the correlates of the three dimensions of job burnout. *Journal of Applied Psychology, 81*(2), 123–133.
McDowall, A., & Kinman, G. (2017). The new nowhere land? A research and practice agenda for the "Always On Culture". *Journal of Organizational Effectiveness: People and Performance, 4*(3), 256–266.
Panaccio, A., Donia, M., Saint-Michel, S., & Liden, R. C. (2015). Servant leadership and wellbeing. In *Flourishing in Life, Work and Careers*. Edward Elgar.
Peccei, R., & Voorde, K. (2019). Human resource management–Well-being–Performance research revisited: Past, present, and future. *Human Resource Management Journal, 29*(4), 539–563.
Peterlin, J. (2016). Incorporation of sustainability into leadership development. *Economic and Business Review, 18*(1).
Pradhan, P., Costa, L., Rybski, D., Lucht, W., & Kropp, J. (2017). A systematic study of Sustainable Development Goal (SDG) interactions. *Earth's Future, 5*(11), 1169–1179.
Pucker, K. P. (2021, May–June). Overselling sustainability reporting. *Harvard Business Review*.
Quirk, H., Crank, H., Carter, A., Leahy, H., & Copeland, R. (2018). Barriers and facilitators to implementing workplace health and wellbeing services in the NHS from the perspective of senior leaders and wellbeing practitioners: A qualitative study. *BMC Public Health, 18*.

Roche, M., & Haar, J. M. (2013). Leaders life aspirations and job burnout: A self-determination theory approach. *Leadership & Organization Development Journal, 34*(6), 515–531.

Schmidt-Traub, G., Kroll, C., Teksoz, K., Durand-Delacre, D., & Sachs, J. (2017). National baselines for the Sustainable Development Goals assessed in the SDG Index and Dashboards. *Nature Geoscience, 10*(8), 547–555.

Swider, B. W., & Zimmerman, R. D. (2010). Born to burnout: A meta-analytic path model of personality, job burnout, and work outcomes. *Journal of Vocational Behavior, 76*(3), 487–506.

United Nations (U.N.). (2015). *Transforming our world: The 2030 Agenda for Sustainable Development*. https://sustainabledevelopment.un.org/post2015/transformingourworld

Urrila, L. I. (2021). From personal wellbeing to relationships: A systematic review on the impact of mindfulness interventions and practices on leaders. *Human Resource Management Review*, 100837.

van Dierendonck, D., Haynes, C., Borrill, C., & Stride, C. (2004). Leadership behavior and subordinate well-being. *Journal of Occupational Health Psychology, 9*, 165–175.

Wright, T. A., & Cropanzano, R. (2000). Psychological well-being and job satisfaction as predictors of job performance. *Journal of Occupational Health Psychology, 5*(1), 84–94.

CHAPTER 6

Leading Change by Engaging and Involving

Abstract A key process in the work of post-heroic leaders is leading change. This chapter summarizes the essential learnings from the science of leading organizational change. Three of the most widely known myths about change leadership are challenged using expert research. The chapter also provides examples of post-heroic leadership in action. Interviews with post-heroic leaders demonstrate how they approach development in their organizations and how they facilitate change processes. An emphasis is put on engaging and involving in order to develop a sense of psychological ownership and safety, as well as on feedback and communication.

Keywords Leading change · Engaging · Involving · Organizational change

6.1 Myths and Science of Leading Change

The literature on leading organizational change has been largely dominated by top-down, strategic perspectives on change (Kotter, 2012) which is also characterized by strong emphasis on readiness for (Repovš et al., 2019) and resistance to change (Oreg, 2003); how to deal with change, and maybe even benefit from it (Ford et al., 2008; Waddell & Sohal, 1998). However, with mounting societal and organizational challenges,

M. Škerlavaj, *Post-Heroic Leadership*,
https://doi.org/10.1007/978-3-030-90820-1_6

it does seem that the limits of mainstream change management research are being tested.

One of the crucial questions for change management researchers, leaders, and their organizations is how to orient oneself in the so-called VUCA world (popular term for volatility, uncertainty, complexity, and ambiguity; see, e.g., Bennett and Lemoine (2014) and Mack et al., (2015). Now is a great time to adopt productive patterns of leading change processes offered by post-heroic leadership. This section summarizes some of the key findings from organizational science about managing the processes of change within and around organizations. An important consideration is to understand where this science deviates from established myths about leading change.

The first myth can be spotted in numerous popular writings and claims that change is the only constant. While indeed challenges facing organizations and their members are plentiful, frequent, and deep, the most innovative organizations know how to balance continuity and renewal. A survey by German researchers on a 60-year sample of European insurance companies clearly rejects this myth (Klarner & Raisch, 2013). Historically, the most successful European insurance companies are the ones that have been able to best capture the rhythm between change and stability, between the times of sowing and reaping.

Our own research (Harrison et al., 2019) shows something similar in the film industry. The most successful film studios are those that manage to provide stability and change at the same time. Marvel, for example, hires experienced inexperienced directors. These are key creators who have proven themselves in lower-class films but have no experience with so-called blockbusters. Marvel expects them to bring freshness into the game over and over again, and it gives them a free space for creating. At the same time, each movie must work in harmony with the others, together creating a connected film universe. It draws from the centuries-old tradition of comic book characters that make up the intellectual capital of the organization. Therefore, this organization has solid stability systems that tightly fasten each of the newcomers into its well-oiled mechanism. Marvel has invented ways to sow and reap, explore and exploit at the same time. Post-heroic leadership should understand that modern organizations need both change and stability.

The second myth: as a rule, people are supposed to resist change, so we need to put up a fire under their feet, establish a sense of urgency and the so-called burning platform (Kotter, 2008). The idea of burning platforms has received quite some attention and criticism (Ford et al., 2008; Holm-Nielsen, 2012). Research (Battilana & Casciaro, 2012) shows that with each major change, people are roughly divided into three categories of virtually equivalent size in terms of how change ready or resistant they are (Repovš et al., 2019). A third are those who have their emotional or cognitive reasons against it. A third are those we are in favour for it. And a third is those who are ambivalent.

A productive way of managing change processes is generally one that engages and involves, leading from the ground floor, and not from the balcony. Studies show that it is especially important to invest energy in a group of people who have not yet decided or who have doubts (Battilana & Casciaro, 2012). In the case of smaller type changes, it is important to also invest in those who oppose. In radical change, confrontations do not work, but we must rely upon the network effects of critical mass. Such momentum and movement can only be achieved by inclusive post-heroic leaders as agents of change who are capable of empathizing with the perspective of the other.

In addition, successful agents of change are also able to awaken the growth instead of fixed mindset (Dweck, 2016; Yeager & Dweck, 2020) among their co-workers. When we focus our energy on how each of us can best develop and progress instead of comparing ourselves to others, we are each individually and all together in a better position. Post-heroic leaders should be the ones who nurture and develop growth mindsets among their colleagues.

The third myth states that people are motivated to change either by a carrot or a stick. This outdated logic is also followed by fresh attempts to introduce the so-called new public management in administrations throughout the various parts of the world. Business organizations on the other hand are aware of research findings and the fact that high value-adding business is an increasingly collective sport. This must be followed by action. In the last decade, a significant portion of Fortune 500 companies have moved from individual performance reward systems to high basic remuneration and collective performance reward systems (Cappelli & Tavis, 2016). For important steps forward, we are not motivated by carrots or scared of a stick.

Behavioural science has long known that people are truly driven by purpose, autonomy, and mastery (Dysvik & Kuvaas, 2011; Pink, 2011; Wong et al., 2016). We can expect progress and successful change if we understand what the purpose of the change is, if we are empowered to actively participate in decision-making, and that we grow from it. Otherwise, there is a clear lack of motivation for change. In recent years, another branch of research and practice of motivational science has strengthened; prosociality. Research (Bolino & Grant, 2016; Grant et al., 2011; Škerlavaj et al., 2018) has shown that seeing your contribution is a strong and lasting motivator to change, to persevere despite difficulties, and to create and innovate. Research is also showing that post-heroic leadership can boost prosociality (Xu et al., 2021).

6.2 How do Post-Heroic Leaders Approach Change?

Exercising post-heroic leadership means behaving according to the learnings of change science. Post-heroic leadership is by definition shared and servant. Therefore, post-heroic leaders engage and involve the followers to develop sense of psychological ownership (Pierce et al., 2001, 2003) of the change processes early on. The benefits are manifold. First, more people can pull together more knowledge and other change-relevant resources (Sieger et al., 2013). Second, ideas are more likely to get implemented (Baer & Brown, 2012; Chai et al., 2020) where more key people have been involved. At the same time, post-heroic leadership of change requires time and effort and cannot be executed hastily or in an autocratic manner.

Several examples from interviews with post-heroic leaders demonstrate how they approach change and development processes at both individual and organizational level. Damjan Osredkar, head of the Clinical Department of Child, Adolescent and Developmental Neurology at the Paediatric clinic of the University Medical Centre Ljubljana, recalls about the upbringing pattern through which he developed a growth mindset (Hlača Ferjančič et al., 2019a). When he proudly brought home an excellent elementary school certificate, his grandfather used to ask him how he plans to improve: "*the fact that I was never good enough for my grandfather sometimes frustrated me a lot. I told him that and we joked about it many times*". He extended this growth mindset to his work as a leader:

> Now I think very similarly. You can always improve in practically all things. I disagree with the mindset that you have achieved something and that

there is no way forward or upward. It can be improved at all times. (Hlača Ferjančič et al., 2019a)

In the literature and practice of leadership (Dweck & Yeager, 2019; Han et al., 2019; Keating & Heslin, 2015; Murphy & Reeves, 2019), we deal a lot with the »Growth mindset«. Many of the traditional systems we have in organizations are designed to make people compare themselves to other people and therefore nurture fixed mindsets. Key performance indicators, various forced rankings, decisions about who will be promoted and who will not, and so on, all of this distracts the focus from what is important. What matters for post-heroic leaders is to develop a culture in which people compare themselves to their previous version and keep asking themselves questions such as: "How can I be better?" and "How can I contribute more?". The leap from this comparison with others and competition, to collaboration and a climate of mastery (Černe et al., 2014; Nerstad et al., 2018; Škerlavaj et al., 2019) as we professionally call it, can be painful, but at the same time it can be very productive.

Lucija Sajevec, director of AMZS, roadside assistance and mobility provider, comments on their organization and its business environment (Hlača Ferjančič et al., 2019b):

> We are operating in the service industry, 365 days a year. Because we are operating in an era in which mobility is changing a lot, we dedicate a lot of activities to this and focus especially on people, change and development.

Reflecting upon the leadership of change, winning hearts and minds of the organizational members, she explicates:

> Every change starts with an individual. /…/ That, as leaders, we first start to change ourselves and then involve our co-workers. There's a big impact in both directions here. It is certainly very nice to have the opportunity to draw from each other on a daily basis. (Hlača Ferjančič et al., 2019b)

She uses the well-known metaphor (Raffo, 2013; Sivers, 2010) of shirtless guy dancing alone in trying to create movement to explain how she understands change agency as an act of engaging and involving:

> I brought in some movement, or I could say we started spreading it. When you are implementing changes, this combines a lot of individual activities, a lot of important things. The most crucial thing we did in the beginning is

> that we started to communicate differently. We really focused on all levels of communication more actively, and we tried to bring this communication to lower levels. We have actively introduced not only new tools, but also other possible events and ways to spend more time together. When you are creating a movement, you must get people on board first. So, we have spent a lot of time internally in the past five years. Our pace is always dictated by our members and the needs of our customers, so we did all this to improve our services. (Hlača Ferjančič et al., 2019b)

Sajevec also agrees with the notion that post-heroic leaders need to balance stability and change:

> Changes are taking place in the business context, and here it is of key importance to prepare people for change quickly enough. We work in mobility. However, mobility is changing, so it is important that we do not make changes quickly overnight, but that we all start preparing for them early enough. A lot of changes await us in the future, from changing professions to changing business models, and I think it is definitely right to take care of employees first. (Hlača Ferjančič et al., 2019b)

Research (Hinojosa et al., 2014; Wu & Parker, 2016) shows that the presence of a leader who engages and involves people in projects that help make sense and motivate on a daily basis is what ensures that changes come to life.

Such leaders also help to develop some psychological ownership of ideas that may not be a product of an individual themselves, but they are willing to take them over and implement them as well. Post-heroic leaders employ a set of organizational practices that connect across the organization and overcome the deficiencies of social categorization (Tajfel et al., 1971). Sajevec lists a number of such practices:

> Right now, are hosting development days. This means bringing ten groups of 40 employees to Ljubljana for a full-day event. Those are employees of various business units. Why? We have noticed that we do not know each other very well, and that we may not only be able to help each other, but also understand each other more easily by knowing our different activities. As a company we are carrying out different activities, not just one, and this understanding and knowledge of each other's environment is crucial. All the connections are good for understanding, and it all stems from there. I think the key is to do it slowly, to talk to each other, to do something

> wrong very often, but to notice it quickly and then take a step back. I see this as important. (Hlača Ferjančič et al., 2019b)

Similar to Damjan Osredkar, also Lucija Sajevec sees her role as a post-heroic leader to serve as facilitator in employee development. She proudly exemplifies:

> When I arrived, Jure was a mechanic, then he was the technical director, and today he is the head of the entire service business, which means he is the product manager. He is making great progress and I think he can take an even higher position in the future. He is well acquainted with the activity and has learned many other things in addition. I could list quite a few more stories. That's what makes me love going to work each morning. (Hlača Ferjančič et al., 2019b)

At the organizational level, Lucija Sajevec reflects upon several demanding change processes and how they dealt with various attitudes towards change:

> We renovated our information system, which was a serious obstacle considering that we have changed it several times in the last 10 years. Here, too, we tried to put a lot into communication and to strengthen our staff. This is such an introduction, where you can always do everything right, but there is still something to fix. But I think it's crucial that people perceive that something is going well. To get back the stability, the feedback loop. We also had a reorganization, systematization and prepared a new salary system. This is also a big change, but we carried out this transition very nicely through one-on-one conversations. (Hlača Ferjančič et al., 2019b)

Indeed, throughout any given process of change, at the micro-psychological level, we transition through four main phases (Burns, 1993). From starting to realize that change is happening, to becoming motivated for it, to having some first experience with it, and finally to adopt it.

Lucija Sajevec also comments on communication as a tool for creating involvement:

> The feedback loop seems to be the key. For everything we do, we try to make sure it doesn't stay in a restricted space. This still sometimes happens, but our efforts are to prevent that from happening. For example, when we carried out »hackathons« with all employees involved, in last

> year's development days, we really focused on how to communicate the status of an individual idea through the internal newsletter. Because we often hear: "Oh, we've suggested something so many times, but nothing has changed«. Today I was talking to a gentleman who is retiring after 42 years at our company. 42 years, that is a really big set of experiences. Past, present. That is why it is all the more important to say back with arguments: "It was good, but now we can look into how we can include and change something". Every vote can count. This also gives everyone some responsibility. This creates a responsibility shared between more people and the more people know about a matter, the easier it is. (Hlača Ferjančič et al., 2019b)

On a similar note, explaining how involvement creates engagement:

> At the end of the year, we invite employees to a final meeting, where we present not only the results of the existing year, but also what awaits us in the coming year. Above all, we build on strengthening leaders so that they are able to discuss with employees, in developmental annual interviews, not only about their career development, but also about what is the commitment and responsibility of each individual in the current year. We are working to communicate the key topics of the year to our employees. I think it's good to repeat these things several times, because sometimes it might go by too quickly and it is worth repeating the key points several times. (Hlača Ferjančič et al., 2019b)

Ms. Sajevec was also open and realistic enough to acknowledge some challenges and problems during the digital transformation:

> In our experience, younger generations are embracing these digital technological changes faster, easier. We have a very diverse age structure, and it is very nice to see the younger employees help the older ones. We had one project last year where we were learning about electronic media as well as various modern social networks. With "diginers" (digital webinars) we also made sure that we were educated within this work and passed this knowledge on to each other. I think it's good to find more fun ways and tools to bring these things closer. If the user sees added value, they will accept any change more quickly. Fortunately, people are different, but if a change is good and it is good for most, then I believe that even the handful who are doubtful at first will come on board sooner or later. (Hlača Ferjančič et al., 2019b)

The experience of leading organizations that have succeeded in digital transformations is supportive of her claims. It is necessary to make sure that organizations have acquired expert knowledge, and at the same time, it is crucial that we do not forget anyone behind when we take care of the digital literacy. Much better results are achieved by organizations that have embarked on the transformation holistically by first setting up the culture (Fandel-Meyer et al., 2017; Hartl & Hess, 2017; Rowles & Brown, 2017; Tomat & Trkman, 2019) and only then setting up technology, and the ones that accomplished this across the entire organization, not through some isolated dedicated departments at the top floor of the organization.

References

Baer, M., & Brown, G. (2012). Blind in one eye: How psychological ownership of ideas affects the types of suggestions people adopt. *Organizational Behavior and Human Decision Processes, 118.*

Battilana, J., & Casciaro, T. (2012). Change agents, networks, and institutions: A contingency theory of organizational change. *Academy of Management Journal, 55*, 381–398.

Battilana, J., & Casciaro, T. (2013). Overcoming resistance to organizational change: Strong ties and affective cooptation. *Management Science, 59*, 819–836.

Battilana, J., & Casciaro, T. (2013). The network secrets of great change agents. *Harvard Business Review, 91*(62–68), 132.

Bennett, N., & Lemoine, J. (2014). What VUCA really means for you. *Harvard Business Review, 92*(1/2).

Bolino, M., & Grant, A. (2016). The bright side of being prosocial at work, and the dark side, too: A review and agenda for research on other-oriented motives, behavior, and impact in organizations. *The Academy of Management Annals, 10*, 1–94.

Burns, D. J. (1993). Adoption decision making process: A pilot study of effects of psychological needs. *Journal of Business and Psychology, 8*(2), 199–213.

Cappelli, P., & Tavis, A. (2016). The performance management revolution. *Harvard Business Review, 94*(10), 58–67.

Chai, D. S., Song, J. H., & You, Y. (2020). Psychological ownership and openness to change: The mediating effects of work engagement, and knowledge creation. *Performance Improvement Quarterly, 33.*

Dweck, C. (2016). What having a "growth mindset" actually means. *Harvard Business Review, 13*, 213–226.

Dweck, C., & Yeager, D. (2019). Mindsets: A View from Two Eras. Perspectives on Psychological Science, 14.

Dysvik, A., & Kuvaas, B. (2011). Intrinsic motivation as a moderator on the relationship between perceived job autonomy and work performance. *European Journal of Work and Organizational Psychology, 20*, 367–387.

Fandel-Meyer, T., Zipp, J., & Schneider, C. (2017). Learning & development in times of digital transformation: Facilitating a culture of change and innovation. *International Journal of Advanced Corporate Learning, 10*, 22.

Ford, J., Ford, L., & D'Amelio, A. (2008). Resistance to change: The rest of the story. *Academy of Management Review, 33*(2), 362–377.

Grant, A., Berry, J., Gino, F., Henifin, T., Myers, C., Brien, M., & Whelan, M. (2011). The necessity of others is the mother of invention: Intrinsic and prosocial motivations, perspective taking, and creativity. *Academy of Management Journal, 54*, 73–96.

Han, S. J., Jin, B., & Oh, J. (2019). *Exploring team growth and fixed mindsets in work teams at a large Korean corporation.* Paper presented at the Adult Education Research Conference, Buffalo, NY.

Harrison, S., Carlsen, A., & Škerlavaj, M. (2019). *Marvel's blockbuster machine.* Harvard Business Review.

Hartl, E., & Hess, T. (2017). *The role of cultural values for digital transformation: Insights from a Delphi study.*

Hinojosa, A., McCauley, K., Randolph-Seng, B., & Gardner, W. (2014). Leader and follower attachment styles: Implications for authentic leader–follower relationships. *The Leadership Quarterly, 25.*

Hlača Ferjančič et al. (2019a). *Vodenje s posluhom 1/5: Od eksperta do vodje.* https://val202.rtvslo.si/2019/12/poslovno-gospodarske-teme-16/

Hlača Ferjančič et al. (2019b). *Vodenje s posluhom 3/5: Sprememba sprememb.* https://val202.rtvslo.si/2020/01/poslovno-gospodarske-teme-18/

Holm-Nielsen, L. B. (2012). Making a strong university stronger: Change without a burning platform. In *Building world-class universities* (pp. 71–87). Brill.

Keating, L., & Heslin, P. (2015). The potential role of mindsets in unleashing employee engagement. *Human Resource Management Review, 25.*

Klarner, P., & Raisch, S. (2013). Move to the beat—Rhythms of change and firm performance. *Academy of Management Journal, 56*(1), 160–184.

Kotter, J. P. (2008). *A sense of urgency.* Harvard Business Press.

Kotter, J. P. (2012). *Leading change.* Harvard Business Publishing.

Mack, O., Khare, A., Kramer, A., & Burgartz, T. (Eds.). (2015). *Managing in a VUCA world.* Springer.

Murphy, M. C., & Reeves, S. L. (2019). Personal and organizational mindsets at work. *Research in Organizational Behavior, 39*, 100121.

Nerstad, C. G. L., Searle, R., Černe, M., Dysvik, A., Škerlavaj, M., & Scherer, R. (2018). Perceived mastery climate, felt trust, and knowledge sharing. *Journal of Organizational Behavior, 39*(4), 429–447.

Oreg, S. (2003). Resistance to change: Developing an individual differences measure. *Journal of Applied Psychology, 88*(4), 680–693.

Pierce, J., Kostova, T., & Dirks, K. (2001). Toward a theory of psychological ownership in organizations. *The Academy of Management Review, 26*, 298.

Pierce, J. L., Kostova, T., & Dirks, K. T. (2003). The state of psychological ownership: Integrating and extending a century of research. *Review of General Psychology, 7*(1), 84–107.

Pink, D. H. (2011). *Drive: The surprising truth about what motivates us*. Penguin.

Raffo, D. (2013). Teaching followership in leadership education. *Journal of Leadership Education, 12*, 262–273.

Repovš, E., Drnovšek, M., & Kaše, R. (2019). Change ready, resistant, or both? Exploring the concepts of individual change readiness and resistance to organizational change. *Economic and Business Review, 21*.

Rowles, D., & Brown, T. (2017). *Building digital culture: A practical guide to successful digital transformation*. Kogan Page Publishers.

Sieger, P., Zellweger, T., & Aquino, K. (2013). Turning agents into psychological principals: Aligning interests of non-owners through psychological ownership. *Journal of Management Studies, 50*, 361–388.

Sivers, D. (2010). *How to start a movement*. TED Talks.

Škerlavaj, M., Connelly, C., Černe, M., & Dysvik, A. (2018). Tell me if you can: Time pressure, prosocial motivation, perspective taking, and knowledge hiding. *Journal of Knowledge Management, 22*, 1489–1509.

Tajfel, H., Billig, M. G., Bundy, R. P., & Flament, C. (1971). Social categorization and intergroup behaviour. *European Journal of Social Psychology, 1*(2), 149–178.

Tomat, L., & Trkman, P. (2019). Digital transformation-the hype and conceptual changes. *Economic and Business Review, 21*(3).

Waddell, D., & Sohal, A. S. (1998). Resistance: A constructive tool for change management. *Management Decision, 36*(8), 543–548.

Wong, S. I., Skerlavaj, M., & Černe, M. (2016). Build coalitions to fit: Autonomy expectations, competence mobilization, and job crafting. *Human Resource Management, 56*.

Wu, C.-H., & Parker, S. K. (2016). The role of leader support in facilitating proactive work behavior: A perspective from attachment theory. *Journal of Management, 43*(4), 1025–1049.

Xu, A. J., Loi, R., & Chow, C. W. C. (2021). Why and when proactive employees take charge at work: The role of servant leadership and prosocial motivation. *European Journal of Work and Organizational Psychology*, 1–11.

Yeager, D., & Dweck, C. (2020). What can be learned from growth mindset controversies? *American Psychologist, 75*, 1269–1284.

Černe, M., Nerstad, C., Dysvik, A., & Skerlavaj, M. (2014). What goes around comes around: Knowledge hiding, perceived motivational climate, and creativity. *The Academy of Management Journal, 57*, 172–192.

Škerlavaj, M., Černe, M., Dysvik, A., Nerstad, C. G. L., & Su, C. (2019). Riding two horses at once: The combined roles of mastery and performance climates in implementing creative ideas. *European Management Review, 16*(2), 285–302.

CHAPTER 7

Building Communities and Collaborative Cultures

Abstract This next chapter merges two interviews with post-heroic leaders from two very different backgrounds. Both discuss the role of leaders as the main builders of community and their role in bringing people together around the shared goal. The creation of a community brings many challenges, from the need to establish shared goals and to build the sense of belonging. Special emphasis is put on the meaning of shared values, collaboration, psychological safety, and the use of feedback and radical candour as a developmental and connecting tool. The interviewees also reflect on dealing with criticism and conflict in an organization.

Keywords Community · Collaboration · Shared goal · Psychological safety · Culture

7.1 Post-Heroic Leaders as Community Builders

It takes a village to be a post-heroic leader as shared leadership is at its very core (Fletcher, 2004). Throughout the interviews we conducted, there was ample evidence of building communities being a recurring pattern of post-heroic leadership behaviours. While this is hardly a surprising finding,

M. Škerlavaj, *Post-Heroic Leadership*,
https://doi.org/10.1007/978-3-030-90820-1_7

it is interesting to observe how post-heroic leaders reflect upon and build their communities.

Building a community starts with galvanizing a group of people around the idea of joint purpose (Bono et al., 2010). Post-heroic leaders are often driven by a higher purpose. As Mic Melanšek, a co-founder of booming scale-up Hooray Studios behind the customized children books Hooray Heroes, stipulates: "*We wanted to create something that we could always present as something good; no matter where we would go, whomever we would have contact with*" (Hlača Ferjančič et al., 2019b).

Dunking Devils is the longest existing acrobatic group of its kind in the world, with continued and growing operations. When talking about Dunking Devils, Domen Rozman, their founding member and director, talks about the community and not about the company. Rozman (Hlača Ferjančič et al., 2019a) reflects upon their growth and attempts to reason why they identify as a community:

> At first, we were a team, then we changed the team into a club. Later, due to the need to carry out major ventures, we established a company. So now we have a company and a society. Ultimately, we then found that these are just two legal entities serving the community. Community is the common denominator, and we are all in the community. From those who work in the office, to someone who comes to training for the first time. We are all parts of the same community. It took quite a while for us all to start realizing this. A legal entity has its purpose only in the context of the organization of business and activities, and community is what we actually build. How do I define a good relationship? One of our guys, Max, who has been around since the beginning, defined it as a modern form of camaraderie. So not camaraderie in the context of socialism, but camaraderie in the sense that when you have a hundred people you just can't be friends with everyone, you can't be a colleague with everyone, but when it comes to doing anything for another, or to strive together towards the same goal, this is a given.

It seems like the reason why Dunking Devils successfully weathered several of the generational transitions is their ability to develop the sense of community and belonging:

> We currently have a lot of people within our community, who have never jumped on a trampoline. We have people in the office who are also part of this community and who would also do anything to help out. They face

> problems such as "You haven't replied to my e-mail, you haven't booked the van, and such". The real challenge is how to deal with someone who is not always in a "life or death" situation, if I exaggerate a bit, how to build our community, so that they will feel the same belonging. Let's say we have on the one hand, a leading acrobat whose function is to do double jumps, and on the other hand, someone whose job it is to find new business opportunities. If they both feel the same degree of belonging to their activity, then within our community they will go through the same filters and the same process. (Hlača Ferjančič et al., 2019a)

Resemblance to the famous Kennedy-janitor encounter at NASA is evident (Carton, 2017). Post-heroic leadership build the sense of community by enhancing the experience of meaning at work.

Furthermore, Andraž Logar, serial entrepreneur and founder of company 3fs, fintech Toshl, and several others, provides an example of community as a business model or an innovation ecosystem. Operating in Slovenia, Scandinavia, and Canada, it has a well-established teleworking system and is setting up spin-off companies. Logar explains how the ecosystem, the community of companies is functioning:

> Each of the four companies went their own way. They have their own directors, their own development teams. We might still share some people with some of them and until recently we have been sharing office spaces, but in 90% they are completely self-contained. 3fs cannot be the one to dictate the development of these companies. We consciously decided that they have to take their own paths, but at the same time, we are very much ready to cooperate. The chances for business cooperation have been opening up now, and by that we will strive to create multiplicative effects in the long run. (Hlača Ferjančič et al., 2020a)

An important element in setting up a successful community and innovation ecosystem is post-heroic leadership. Logar reflects about his leadership role in a servant, humble yet direct way:

> I think being your own boss sounds very romantic. In reality, the boss' bosses are usually their employees or their clients. Our company does not have a hierarchical architecture. Maybe, according to the bureaucracy, but in reality, the bosses are in some way employed by their employees. (Hlača Ferjančič et al., 2020a)

Anka Lipuščcek Miklavič is the long-standing director of a local dairy farm in the picturesque Soča Valley region and reflects upon her 14 years at the helm of the company. When asked about the reasons for their success in weathering some difficult times she immediately turns to the community:

> Firstly, I have to tell you that WE succeeded. Not only me, but WE succeeded. And I think the reason for our success and what drove us forward was the awareness that we are not working only for ourselves, but for all of us; for the people of our region, who were then tied to Mlekarna Planika, to the Agricultural Cooperative Tolmin. The beginnings were extremely difficult. We were a blank page with no market, no knowledge, after all no special technologies, no products. Back then, we entered the market as the ninth dairy company and you know what it's like to come as a newcomer, one that no one knows. It was terribly difficult to come to an agreement with the retailers to get even just a tiny bit of space in the refrigerator shelves, and then we had to roll up our sleeves and work to the maximum so that we could succeed. (Hlača Ferjančič et al., 2020b)

Mrs. Lipuščcek Miklavič reflects further upon the involvement in the local environment as a driver of responsible, post-heroic leadership:

> We all know each other. The valley is small. There aren't very many people there. So once a director of a very large company told me: "Anka, why do you care at all, if it doesn't work out, you can simply leave." But, I can only go to Tolmin, where I live and where everyone knows me. This is one great responsibility to those employed in the dairy and to those tied to it, who are dependent on it; it is our owners, our farmers and in the end ourselves. After all, if it didn't work out or if we went into the wrong direction, it would show, not only on myself, so to speak, but also on my family, on my children. Sometimes I joke that I have wide shoulders, so I can then carry all of that burden. (Hlača Ferjančič et al., 2020b)

In particular, when dealing with obstacles, servant and shared nature of post-heroic leadership shows:

> I'll be honest. Sometimes it doesn't work out the way one would like because of some boundaries on one side or another. But what I think is important is that you talk to people, communicate with them; that if someone has a problem, they expose it and then you try to solve it together. (Hlača Ferjančič et al., 2020b)

7.2 Post-Heroic Leaders as Anchors of Collaborative Culture

As far as the other dimension of post-heroic leadership, servant leadership is concerned, Covey (2006) argues that genuine servant leaders are those that evoke servant leadership in others. Post-heroic leadership is therefore as much servant as it is shared and demonstrates through various approaches towards building a collaborative culture.

Domen Rozman, the leader of the acrobatic group Dunking Devils, explains the process through which they are developing a collaborative culture:

> We have three core values that we acquired and then later also wrote down. The first is that we cultivate teamwork as a value in itself. We were, in a way, forced into this because of the nature of this sport. There are only one ball and one basket, and six people have to pass that one ball. Regardless of who throws the ball through the hoop, it is very clear whether we won or not. Another equally important issue is our motto: "there is only one right direction: upwards". Progress is the guide. We all strive for progress together and we clearly know what that progress is, this is what connects us. The third thing is, that one of our values is the experience. Whatever we do, it must be a positive experience for the viewers, and at the same time, every experience must represent growth for us. Awareness of these three values and returning to them on a weekly, monthly basis is what connects us at a very deep level. (Hlača Ferjančič et al., 2019a)

Damjan Osredkar (Hlača Ferjančič et al., 2019a) also talks about the importance of leaders setting up psychological safety (Edmondson, 1999; Edmondson & Lei, 2014; Frazier et al., 2017). So does Domen Rozman, leader of the world-renowned acrobatic team the Dunking Devils, when he explains their team dynamics and the concept of "affectionate teasing":

> To expose one's weakness means expecting that weakness, working on it, and knowing that the team will cover your back. This all builds a deep level of trust. Precisely trust and sincerity is something that ties the deep connections. /…/ It is important to tease each other and make jokes in the context of achieving a higher goal and sincere relationships. Without affectionate teasing our relationships would remain superficial. (Hlača Ferjančič et al., 2019a)

He further explicates how Dunking Devils in a similar fashion to Pixar's idea of radical candour (Catmull, 2008; Scott, 2019) strike a thin line between harsh feedback and feedback as a developmental and connecting tool:

> A group of boys who spend a lot of time together, they are sure to start teasing each other at some point. This can be very negative. However, if you put that into the context of a team committed to one common goal, then with that joking and teasing, you expose each other's weaknesses. When I point out someone's weakness and we can both laugh about it, through that I tell them that I accept them despite this weakness, and they accept their weakness as such, work on it, or know that the team will take over what they cannot do; that is building a deep level of trust. This level of trust and sincerity is what forms close ties. It is important that we make fun of each other, but in the context of some higher goal and in the context of establishing sincere relationships. If we just pat each other on the back and say that we are all perfect and that everything is fine, then our relationships remain superficial. (Hlača Ferjančič et al., 2019a)

And the ball does not end up in the basket.

Domen Rozman explains how post-heroic leaders should help their teams deal with mistakes and learn from them:

> When things don't go smoothly, we always talk about it. But it depends on whether it requires a conversation between me and one of the main members, or whether it requires a conversation between me and someone half my age. When it comes to major systemic matters, we have regular community meetings to which all members are invited and where we discuss hot topics. We have also implemented other approaches. As an example, two years ago, when we opened the Woop trampoline park and filmed the Fly Guys series with Hollywood in parallel. At the time, 15 key members were involved in these two projects, and it was absolutely clear to us that one project opens a window to Hollywood and another project gives the best possible conditions here. We were so focused, and it seemed logical to us that the younger members would just patiently wait no matter what. Because we were not there, there were no performances and because we were without a place to practice for three months in the transition period. (Hlača Ferjančič et al., 2019a)

> When this all was over, we started seeing that things were not going well in the community, and we did a really drastic thing. We opened an anonymous survey with questions asking what was good, what would need to be changed, to the point when other members could anonymously expose us, who were leading. We wrote down what we did wrong and what they would have done differently. The survey was active for 14 days, so it was filled out by all members, after which we had an internal meeting where we discussed everything together and put our emotions aside. (Hlača Ferjančič et al., 2019a)

> Then, in a series of four meetings once a week, we cleaned up everything that had accumulated. That is, to zero. This is the most drastic thing we did, or that an organization can do. We have set extremely high standards for what psychological safety means and what good relationships mean. (Hlača Ferjančič et al., 2019a)

Rozman also explains about his personal and leadership role in developing psychological safety in their organization:

> Personally, I am especially prone to noticing such things. However, I am very happy and proud that now other, younger members come to me and tell me, or even sort things out themselves as soon as something at the relationship level starts to go wrong. Because good relationships are the foundation for everything else. We do not tolerate relationships slowly deteriorating. We do not tolerate »ah, it will all be fine«. Sometimes even three months of not-dealing with relationships is enough to bring down a lot of things. (Hlača Ferjančič et al., 2019a)

Similarly, Andraž Logar, from 3fs (Hlača Ferjančič et al., 2020a), reflects about the feedback and criticism:

> I receive criticism about my own actions and the actions of the wider collective. It is necessary to hear it and to respond. Negative criticism always hurts, but if you can't hear it, you can't fix anything either. In entrepreneurship, luck is always needed, and we have had, I think, quite a few of such events. On the first day of starting a company we got the opportunity to work for the most demanding markets in the world. … These people, specifically people from multinationals and from the Scandinavian market, tolerated our stupidity or better, our youth. They gave us constant opportunities and they knew on the basis of which criteria they can judge us. I believe it prevailed that they liked to work with people who

> were, as we would say in Slovene, diligent. And they really like working with people to have the moral and ethical standards in place, so that there are no problems in a business relationship. When they felt we have that, and it seems to me that they gave us quite a lot of time, then we grew with them. This feedback, positive and negative, we also got to some extent from them, from our customers. (Hlača Ferjančič et al., 2020a)

Literature on feedback as a leadership and developmental tool is extensive (Hattie & Timperley, 2007; Kelloway et al., 2000). The lessons from our qualitative research and some previous research (De Dreu, 1997; Mooney et al., 2007) show that post-heroic leaders should not shy away from exposing the cognitive conflict in their collaborative processes, as long as the affective conflict is kept to minimum. Any given complex task (Hærem et al., 2014; Wood, 1986) requires mastering interdependence and dealing with uncertainty and adjusting to conflicting information and even goals group members might have. It is a task of the post-heroic leader to serve as a facilitator and help their team and organization to deal with them.

References

Bono, J. E., Shen, W., & Snyder, M. (2010). Fostering integrative community leadership. *The Leadership Quarterly, 21*(2), 324–335.

Carton, A. M. (2017). "I'm not mopping the floors, I'm putting a man on the moon": How NASA leaders enhanced the meaningfulness of work by changing the meaning of work. *Administrative Science Quarterly, 63*(2), 323–369.

Catmull, E. (2008). *How Pixar fosters collective creativity*. Harvard Business Review.

Covey, S. R. (2006). Servant-leadership and community leadership in the 21st century. *The International Journal of Servant-Leadership, 2*(1), 103–109.

De Dreu, C. K. W. (1997). Productive conflict: The importance of conflict management and conflict issue. *Using conflict in organizations* (pp. 9–22). Sage.

Edmondson, A. (1999). Psychological safety and learning behavior in work teams. *Administrative Science Quarterly, 44*(2), 350–383.

Edmondson, A., & Lei, Z. (2014). Psychological safety: The history, renaissance, and future of an interpersonal construct. *Annual Review of Organizational Psychology and Organizational Behavior, 1*, 23–43.

Fletcher, J. K. (2004). The paradox of postheroic leadership: An essay on gender, power, and transformational change. *The Leadership Quarterly, 15*(5), 647–661.

Frazier, M. L., Fainshmidt, S., Klinger, R. L., Pezeshkan, A., & Vracheva, V. (2017). Psychological safety: A meta-analytic review and extension. *Personnel Psychology, 70*(1), 113–165.

Hattie, J., & Timperley, H. (2007). The power of feedback. *Review of Educational Research, 77*(1), 81–112.

Hlača Ferjančič et al. (2019a). *Vodenje s posluhom 4/5: Od skupine do tima.* https://val202.rtvslo.si/2019/12/poslovno-gospodarske-teme-19/

Hlača Ferjančič et al. (2019b). *Vodenje s posluhom 5/5: Med kreativnostjo in Excelom.* https://val202.rtvslo.si/2019/12/poslovno-gospodarske-teme-20/

Hlača Ferjančič et al. (2020a). *Vodenje s posluhom: Šefi šefa so njegovi zaposleni.* https://val202.rtvslo.si/2020/08/poslovno-gospodarske-teme-40/

Hlača Ferjančič et al. (2020b). *Vodenje s posluhom: Krepitev odpornosti vodij.* https://val202.rtvslo.si/2020/09/poslovno-gospodarske-teme-41/

Hærem, T., Pentland, B., & Miller, K. (2014). Task complexity: Extending a core concept. *The Academy of Management Review, 40*(3), 446–460.

Kelloway, K., Barling, J., & Helleur, J. (2000). Enhancing transformational leadership: The roles of training and feedback. *Leadership & Organization Development Journal, 21*, 145–149.

Mooney, A., Holahan, P., & Amason, A. (2007). Don't take it personally: Exploring cognitive conflict as a mediator of affective conflict. *Journal of Management Studies, 44*, 733–758.

Scott, K. (2019). *Radical candor: Fully revised & updated edition: Be a kick-ass boss without losing your humanity*. St. Martin's Press.

Wood, R. (1986). Task complexity: Definition of the construct. *Organizational Behavior and Human Decision Processes, 37*, 60–82.

PART III

Post-Heroic Leadership Outcomes

In the first two parts of this book, we learnt about the need for healthier and more productive approaches to leadership, called post-heroic leadership. Its' servant and shared nature is better suited to the complex nature of work ahead of us. Readers could also benefit from a rich array of post-heroic leadership experiences, from transitioning into a leadership role, to developing sustainable leadership patterns for employees and leaders alike, to leading change by engaging and involving.

Part III focuses on selected, most salient post-heroic leadership outcomes. Naturally, there are more of them, and I invite the leader to revisit the literature review of post-heroic leadership research in Part I for more complete overview of the previous research.

Chapter 8 links post-heroic leadership to creativity and innovation in the workplace. It examines the role of post-heroic leadership in utilizing innovative working methods as well as development of cultures conducive to innovation.

Chapter 9 addresses resilience and well-being as another set of central outcomes of post-heroic leadership. Chapter 10 provides an epilogue and provides an agenda for future research and action.

CHAPTER 8

Post-Heroic Leadership of Creativity and Innovation: From Idea to Excel

Abstract The chapter deals with the two roles post-heroic leadership has in facilitating creativity and innovation; how to resolve the innovation paradox and ensure continuous innovation. This type of leadership supports innovative behaviours and the implementation of innovative ideas. The chapter also offers insight into understanding how post-heroic leaders help in sustaining creativity and innovation across time through four motivational drivers of creativity—autonomy, mastery, purpose, and prosociality. The interviews presented touch upon post-heroic leadership and continuous innovation in a start-up setting and upon intrapreneurship in mature organizations.

Keywords Leadership · Creativity · Innovation · Innovation paradox · Intrapreneurship · Continuous innovation

Albert Einstein is famously and most likely wrongly attributed to be the author of the thought that "*we can't solve problems by using the same kind of thinking we used when we created them*". Regardless of who the author is, it is an influential saying that calls for need for smarter approaches to problem solving. Might I humbly add, neither can we lead in the same way that has previously contributed to the challenges that we are currently hoping to resolve with creativity and innovation.

M. Škerlavaj, *Post-Heroic Leadership*,
https://doi.org/10.1007/978-3-030-90820-1_8

This chapter is dedicated to the role post-heroic leadership has in stimulating creativity and innovation at work. There are two key questions I would like to invite the readers to explore. First, how can post-heroic leadership help resolve the innovation paradox (Miron-Spektor et al., 2011)—the notion that implementation of ideas often requires different and even opposing approaches compared to idea generation. Second, what kind of cultures for innovation can post-heroic leaders nurture to innovate over and over again?

8.1 Post-Heroic Leadership and Innovative Working Methods

Innovation is inherently a risky endeavour and requires active leadership. Meta-analytical evidence (Damanpour, 1991; Hammond et al., 2011; Rosenbusch et al., 2011) shows a different picture at individual level compared to organizational level. Individuals who are exhibiting more creative and innovative behaviours are also more likely to be higher achievers, more collegiate, and less prone to counter-productive work behaviours. At the organizational level, the association between innovation and performance is moderately positive and highly variant. One of the key factors to turn innovation into performance is leadership.

I argue that post-heroic leadership fulfils many of the requirements to be supportive of innovation processes. As innovation is turning from ideas to implementation, more and more people are involved. With its sharedness and servantship, post-heroic leadership has the capacity of tailoring to the complex tasks (Wood, 1986), which innovative work inherently is.

An important part of the innovation-related risks stems from the nature of the innovation paradox. Behaviours supportive of idea generation are often in opposition to the factors stimulating its implementation. Furthermore, some organizations that place innovation at their core even operate in top management pairs, where complementarity of the pair/top management team members is the key guiding principle. Mic Melanšek (Hlača Ferjančič et al., 2019), co-founder of Hooray Studios, a scaleup in the family entertainment industry, reflects upon his and his co-founders' leadership style strengths, weaknesses, and complementarities:

> It would be very difficult for me to be a leader to someone whom I would need to babysit. I know that is not a virtue I can be proud of, but that is how I function. Even when I hire people, when I invite them into my

team, one of the prerequisites is not having to follow me, but that the only mantra when we get to work in the morning is to do something better, something more, something nicer.

Rado [co-founder] took on a different role. He makes sure that there is a safety net, so that I can do what I want. He handles everything, from the legal and financial, to business partners and so on. And then marketing and the creative parts of the company can work well. We have different views, but luckily, they are very complementary. (Hlača Ferjančič et al., 2019)

Indeed, Krapež Trošt and Škerlavaj (2016) empirically demonstrate that idea generation is a much more affective process compared to idea implementation, which is more cognitive (Krapež Trošt & Škerlavaj, 2016; Krapež Trošt et al., 2016; Škerlavaj et al., 2016). In this dance of creativity and innovation, the romantic side of creating ideas and the endless imagination must coincide with the hard side where the Excel has to work, where the resources need to be available and where the things have to be on time. In short, this dance between the two complementary sides of creativity and innovation is vital, and it is also the situation in which many companies slip on the dance floor. Apparently, Hooray Studios thrives on this.

The above-mentioned study among teams in German research and development organizations found that the heart is more important for generating ideas and the head for their implementation. Intuition is what drives the creative part, thinking outside the box. While the rational-cognitive side is the one that is more decisive in the implementation of these ideas.

In all of the above, knowledge on innovative working methods and the creation of innovative business models can also be of great help to us. As Einstein said, different times require different solutions. If we can rely on traditional project management methods, Gantt charts and milestones in routine tasks, this is not ideal for complex tasks. A family of innovation techniques is of much greater help; from the innovator method (Furr & Dyer, 2014), design thinking, through agile and lean methods, to the canvas of business models (Ostenwalder & Pigneur, 2010).

All of these methods and techniques (Furr & Dyer, 2014) have three things in common. The first one is that they arise from an in-depth understanding of user needs. It is not about what the expert thinks the user needs. It is about the decision-maker taking enough time to really understand the need as well. The second feature is iterativeness. In fact, all modern methods of work suitable for "wicked" problems use the same logic that we have always used in science. We move from the smallest to the largest, from the sample to the population, relying on testing hypotheses with the best tools and methods available to us. Once we have the proof, we move on. The third feature is experimentation. If we don't know if our ideas stand up to judgement or not, we need to be prepared to learn from mistakes and make quick turns based on what we have learned.

An important empirical question is—what role do post-heroic leadership behaviours have in facilitating those innovative working methods and approaches. Melanšek explains the iterativeness and experimentation behind the development of their successful scale-up. It all started with several trial and errors:

> For the first three years, everything was very much in its infancy, quite modest. We did business in Slovenia with small experiments abroad. We wanted to go to Austria, but it didn't work out, because Austrians are still more like Germans than like Slovenes. We wanted to go to Croatia, but it didn't work out. Croats are obviously less like Slovenes than we thought they were. So, we pulled back from those markets. This was a very smart move.
>
> We were just about to close the company. I was traveling the world at the time. Rado came to the other end of the world to meet me. We sat down for a beer and wondered if we were going to give it one more try or if that was the moment we would go back to work for someone else. And when you say that sentence out loud, that you're going to go back to working for someone else, you see that it sounds silly. And we said let's try some more. And we tried a little more, we tried to approach things in a smarter way. (Hlača Ferjančič et al., 2019)

An important learning that Rado and Mic reached was that creative ideas need to be joined with hard numbers and facts:

> For the first three years, you think you're very creative and innovative and forget about the Excel, both in a metaphorical and physical sense. So, we started to deal with numbers a bit more to validate our business model. We went to Germany and made a breakthrough in that market. We found our place in the market alongside three providers of similar books. Since then, things have escalated very quickly. In the last three years, we have grown from two unemployed, me and Rado, who did not have a salary. At first, we were overworked and yet unemployed, and now there are over 100 of

> us. We are now present in seven markets, and I think we are expanding into new markets in a smart and organic way. (Hlača Ferjančič et al., 2019)

Our qualitative data therefore shows how post-heroic leadership is helping to deal with the innovation paradox. Readers will be aware that it is by no means a simple act and that there are trade-offs involved that require mastery of innovative working methods. Mr. Melanšek explains the tensions he and his company experience when dealing with the innovation paradox:

> We are dealing with [the innovation paradox] right now. We are enforcing some processes on the top of creativity, and it hurts me a lot. This is very unnatural to me, but the results already show that it is a much better approach. Not only faster, but also more cost effective. You have some resources you can reuse, for instance. However, I am still committed to freedom at any stage of the product's creation. If we find we've done something wrong on a product that is 90 percent finished, we must be able to admit it and say that it is bad. It can't happen that we cannot start from scratch, or go back to 60 percent, just because we got to 90 percent and the processes say we need to finish now. (Hlača Ferjančič et al., 2019)

To understand creativity under constraints, one has to understand the process and the context in which innovation takes place. Mr. Melanšek explains the process of creating a book and how they deal with tensions between autonomy and structure in leading such a process:

> We go through several stages when creating a book. There is a basic idea that goes through an incubation phase, which means that you only think, dream about it. It doesn't even need to be put on paper; it just somehow matures. Then there is the phase of internal preparation, where we have internal illustrators, authors, editors, project managers, where we put the matter in such a mature form that we can attract those who will actually carry out the project. So first we have some rough sketches, then the illustrator takes over; first we have a synopsis and then we create the main texts. We used to do all of this more with our hearts, we were making quick judgements on whether something was wrong or not. But now we are present in so many markets and we have such big plans that we need to get this phase over as soon as possible and move on to the second phase. Still, within the phase, we try to be very open. (Hlača Ferjančič et al., 2019)

Mr. Melanšek is also very much aware of the fact that dealing with the innovation paradox is not a one-time-off deal. It is a repetitive phenomenon and is therefore strongly related to the organizational culture:

> We are already at a point when this can also become a kind of pain in the firm. Mainly because you need to extend this mentality, not only to your immediate employees, but also to your external partners. However, I believe that if a company has this, it can stay healthy. (Hlača Ferjančič et al., 2019)

8.2 Post-Heroic Leadership and Innovative Organizational Cultures

Our second topic of interest will be dedicated to understanding how post-heroic leaders can help in sustaining creativity and innovation across time. In other words, how can post-heroic leaders help in creating organizational cultures in support of sustained innovation. After all, innovation is an example of complex tasks (Hærem, Pentland, & Miller, 2014) that require for post-heroic leaders to deal with both interdependence and uncertainty.

From decades of research on motivational drivers of creativity and innovation (Pink, 2011), we can reasonably expect that post-heroic leadership will be an excellent fit to support development of innovative organizational cultures. They include autonomy, mastery, purpose (Dysvik & Kuvaas, 2011; Pink, 2011; Wong et al., 2016), and prosociality (Bolino & Grant, 2016; Grant et al., 2011). Both shared and servant dimensions of post-heroic leadership are likely to support development of organizational cultures that are inductive to continuous innovation. Let us explore qualitative data and learn about the manifestations of post-heroic leadership related to innovation.

Mic Melanšek explains his beliefs on what kind of organizational culture is contributing to continuous innovation:

> I believe we need to have a good time at the firm. Opening markets, making products that challenge the whole company, that are fun and that we enjoy. It has to be like that. This permeates the company as such and at the same time lets all employees know that it is allowed and also desirable.

> Today we're talking about innovation and creativity and that is definitely something you can't do with a serious face. (Hlača Ferjančič et al., 2019)

Many organizations that are experiencing rapid growth, extensive, and fast hiring and emphasize the strength of their culture as a crucial lever of continued innovation will recognize themselves in the following story:

> I can tell where we also made a mistake. Exactly two years ago, a season opened for us, namely Father's Day, which is not as popular in Slovenia as elsewhere. The big number of orders surprised us a lot at the time and even crashed the firm a bit. Our processes have failed because they were not prepared for such a volume and at that time we were hiring quite recklessly. /.../ Back then we needed people with some specific knowledge like language skills, design knowledge.
>
> We nodded to everyone, we hired too recklessly, and half a year later, as we entered the second season, it became very clear that many of these individuals did not come to the firm at the right time to feel the right culture. Because our culture is creative after all, our culture is not reactive to the demand that comes by itself, we create products to create demand. They came in during that golden period when everything was flourishing, everything was great, there was too much of everything. We've had trouble for quite some time to, I won't say rehabilitate, because it sounds ugly, but we've told people anyway that it is not self-evident that they have a job and that we can give them a salary. (Hlača Ferjančič et al., 2019)

Therefore, the company learnt about the importance of cultural and competence fit:

> We try much harder to hire people who understand this. I'm not saying a person should be grateful to have a job, but still some general gratitude for having a nice job, having nice co-workers, having a peaceful life. That has to be present, I still have it too. We also try to hire people who already have some experience. Previously, we said: "You don't have to have experience, just that you're very enthusiastic." This is great, but it's not enough. (Hlača Ferjančič et al., 2019)

A quite an interesting observation for the interview data is that, at Hooray Studios, they are aware of the simultaneous need for diversity and continuity. They employ people from all over the world but also encourage the creative core to be collocated:

> We strive to ensure that everyone who works for us is in Ljubljana. Meaning that we don't have offices anywhere else where people would work for us. With the exception of the printing facilities, we have eight worldwide. They are not our printing houses, but they are very strong business partners, which means that we are practically like connected companies. People in the office come from eight or nine countries, so mostly we communicate in English. (Hlača Ferjančič et al., 2019)
>
> Our wish is to bring as many of our employees to Slovenia as possible, which takes a lot of time. Even from the viewpoint of bureaucracy, unfortunately, is not entirely clear how to solve this. The company itself is divided very similarly to an advertising agency. We have one product, and we do everything inhouse. We don't outsource anything. This has been my idea from the beginning, and I insist on it. All texts, all photo material, video material, production, customer support, everything must be within the company, or as much as possible, except in some really high demand seasons, when we really cannot do it alone. (Hlača Ferjančič et al., 2019)

At the stage in which Hooray Studios are right now, being a scale-up, a very good approximation of culture is to understand the values, beliefs, and characteristics founders have themselves. Reflecting upon his own leadership style and the one of co-founder Mr. Rado Daradan, Mr. Melanšek identifies and important lesson about cultures in support of continuous innovation. They are paradoxical themselves. On the one hand, they nurture change, and on the other, they secure stability (Harrison et al., 2019). Just like Mr. Melanšek is seeing both of the Hooray Studios founders and their complementarities as leaders:

> He [Rado] is still very focused on stability, again I am saying this a little bit on his behalf, but I think it brings him peace. It seems to me that this is his virtue, that he wants to have things under control. I don't need to have them under control, or the less I have, the happier I am. He probably pays his phone bills regularly, and I pay them very irregularly because that's the last thing I think of. He has some areas that don't sound innovative at first glance, that is far from the truth. Financial or legal approaches can also be very innovative fields. (Hlača Ferjančič et al., 2019)

Reflecting upon experiences in the employee selection interviews, Mr. Melanšek provides a rather interesting observation on the creativity and innovation perceptions among prospective employees:

> In the beginning, I was very careful when someone came in for an interview and said: “I am a very creative person”. That’s very easy to say and a person is very offended if you tell them that they are not creative. On the other hand, a person is not very offended if you tell them: "You don’t know how to work in Excel". Anyone would say: “Yes, I really don’t know Excel, I don’t really like to work in it, but I’m very creative.” We are very careful to try, not to really measure creativity, but not to blindly succumb to anyone who says: “I am creative.” (Hlača Ferjančič et al., 2019)

As it is often the case with start-ups growing toward scaleups, the need for systematic human resource management came post-hoc. In a humble manner, Mr. Melanšek reflects upon his own shortcomings as a leader:

> My weakness is that I don’t deal with people enough. But when I consider whether it is better to develop new products, which I usually do with a limited team, or to work with a wider team, to me it is more important to have my own inner circle of people, whom I trust very much and I can create with. Now I think we are well on our way to knowing how we are going to tackle things in the future because we are putting things into certain processes and these processes very clearly indicate the need for employment. It is important that you don’t hire recklessly, but that you know how to determine very precisely where you are missing a person for what job. You can’t just leave it to guessing. (Hlača Ferjančič et al., 2019)

Faced with a mental experiment to choose either someone that fits into their culture, but does not yet have much knowledge, and someone who is experienced but does not fit into the culture, Mic Melanšek comments:

> If we do choose the second one, they will lose the job quite soon. /…/ There are 120 of us now. We are on two floors, and if something negative starts happening in one department on the other floor it is very difficult to contaminate it if it spreads too much. I think we have all things set up so well that if there is some dissatisfaction it is just as much the fault of that individual as it is the fault of the company. We are no guiltier than they are and here it is very logical that you go your separate ways, just like in any relationship. If we are both equally dissatisfied, let’s go our separate ways. If a person does not have the expertise and fits in to the culture, it depends a little on which department they work in. It is definitely possible to educate them, we encourage and finance education if necessary, but it

> again depends on the individual whether they want it or not. It is not self-evident that someone you pay for schooling will do it and then be more knowledgeable. Here I have no answer. (Hlača Ferjančič et al., 2019)

In reality, the dilemma of hiring for cultural or experience fit is one that post-heroic leaders would like to avoid. Following employee recruitment and selection, the next crucial tool for building cultures supportive of continuous innovation is onboarding and socializing (Bauer & Erdogan, 2011; Saks et al., 2007; Sluss & Thompson, 2012):

> All employees we bring to Slovenia are already tested by us. Which means someone is already working well enough remotely that if they can keep their work at that level, that would be okay. I see only one strong indicator in favour of the office, to make them feel our culture of creation. Every day we talk about how many books we have sold in which markets and whether Italy is better than Germany, to have some healthy competition. A bit of fun. But it is always overwhelming because you see people coming in the morning and staying maybe even later, sometimes we even have some drinks at the office after work. You don't have that if you're out of the office. Now, to believe that someone who will come to us will progress personally or progress professionally, I am not an arbiter of this, nor can I influence it. It will be up to them to decide whether they want that or not. But I know that with this knowledge they have, they are more than good enough to come to us. (Hlača Ferjančič et al., 2019)

We learned about post-heroic leadership and continuous innovation in a start-up/scaleup setting. Leaders in large and mature organizations have quite different degrees of freedom in developing their cultures. Still, large multinational organizations are becoming increasingly aware that they heavily depend upon the innovation, that culture is the key to continued success, and they bet on intrapreneurship (Antoncic & Hisrich, 2001, 2003; Desouza, 2011). Birkinshaw (2019) counters the common conviction, carefully analyses the last 25-year developments in Future 500 list of the companies, to learn than only 17 of them are actual newcomers. Therefore, it is crucial for us to understand what post-heroic leaders in mature organizations are doing with their cultures to sustain innovation.

Danfoss is a successful Danish family business that employs more than 38,000 people globally. They are the world's leading suppliers of products for energy-efficient remotely operated heating and cooling solutions and air conditioning for buildings. They are especially proud of their inclusive culture and hackathons, events where employees from different departments solve a specific challenge or task in a given time frame.

Mateja Panjan, front-end and innovation manager at Danfoss, explains their approach towards innovation and new ways of working in general:

> Five years ago, we set up a special department at Danfoss called "Future of Work", where we gather employees from different departments, from different parts of the world and together we think about how we could change the organization, connect it more, involve employees more. Above all, we want to implement open innovation, employee connectedness, and here we have created quite a few very interesting practices in the last five years, such as internal hackathons, talent exchange between companies, "reverse mentoring". In short, these are all new ways of working that somehow connect the organization and make us a little more open to new ways of working. (Hlača Ferjančič et al., 2020)

Large organizations anywhere in the world are aiming to capitalize on their scale. Large systems have their advantages and many opportunities to learn from each other, but at the same time they are discovering the need to gain the agility that small systems have. Several practices described above are approaches towards complementing strengths of large systems with those of smaller organizations, start-ups for example.

Ms. Panjan explains how the intrapreneurship is built as a part of the culture of involvement (Prieto et al., 2020) in their organization:

> We have been encouraging employees that their employer will not build their careers, but that each is responsible for developing their own careers. Employees have to show some initiative, to join these internal projects and work like an entrepreneur who wants to build something new. Five years ago, we started implementing these internal hackathons. We organize them in various areas, from organizational development, R&D, to the development of new technologies. During a hackathon in February, we were figuring out how blockchain technology could benefit our way of working and our existing technologies. (Hlača Ferjančič et al., 2020)

> These hackathons are a kind of quick checks, quick experiments to see with the customer, what works well and what doesn't, and at the same time to change the process of innovation. So far, this process has been very traditional. It has taken us about two years to develop a new product, but now we are making a prototype as soon as possible, and showing it to the customer, to get that feedback as soon as possible and make improvements.

> The real magic happens when you put employees from different parts of the organization together to solve an individual challenge and they bring in the knowledge they have. (Hlača Ferjančič et al., 2020)

Ms. Panjan adds that an important part of the success in hackathons is to stay open to the external perspectives and actively work with students and universities on real-life challenges the company faces:

> We love to work with students, too. I would like to highlight the latest experience. This was the summer school tackling digitalization, organized with the School of Economics and Business, University of Ljubljana. Working together with three international students was a great experience, and together we came up with a nice solution in the field of gamification, to enhance the competencies of our salespeople. We are thinking of continuing the story together with these students, to develop the project further with them. (Hlača Ferjančič et al., 2020)

Due to their popularity, hackathons have been under some scrutiny for the effect they have on culture and other relevant long-term factors (Briscoe, 2014; Chan et al., 2020; Decker et al., 2015; Nolte et al., 2020). While they contribute to idea generation and create joy in the moment, their translation into innovation and longer-term effects on culture is not guaranteed. Post-heroic leaders are aware of the need to combine the hype of hackathons into existing organizational systems, structures, and culture:

> At the very beginning they were organized only for fun, as we started building this innovative connecting culture. Later we got some feedback, that it is not nice to see the ideas were later not implemented. Now we are doing things in a more guided, structured manner. It is also true that we somehow generate quite a few ideas in the organization and for some of them it is not the right time. We put those aside, but for those that make sense and are suitable at the time, we pick them up and develop them further. (Hlača Ferjančič et al., 2020)

Ms. Panjan further explicates the importance of feedback and psychological safety in developing an innovative culture:

> At Danfoss, we are trying to establish a kind of "innovation for all" culture; we have a platform where every employee can write down their ideas and others from all over the world can monitor or upgrade them. They can like and comment on an idea. In this way we give ideas transparency and even

if it is not the right time to develop someone's idea in China, for example, maybe a colleague in Poland will take it and develop it there. We have a transparent option that make it possible for an idea to be used by anyone. (Hlača Ferjančič et al., 2020)

References

Antoncic, B., & Hisrich, R. (2001). Intrapreneurship: Construct refinement and cross-cultural validation. *Journal of Business Venturing, 16*, 495–527.

Antoncic, B., & Hisrich, R. (2003). Clarifying the intrapreneurship concept. *Journal of Small Business and Enterprise Development, 10*, 7–24.

Bauer, T., & Erdogan, B. (2011). Organizational socialization: The effective onboarding of new employees. In *APA handbook of I/O psychology* (Vol. 3, pp. 51–64). American Psychological Association.

Birkinshaw, J. (2019). Digital disruption—The power of nuance and the dangers of extrapolation. *Forbes*.

Bolino, M., & Grant, A. (2016). The bright side of being prosocial at work, and the dark side, too: A review and agenda for research on other-oriented motives, behavior, and impact in organizations. *The Academy of Management Annals, 10*, 1–94.

Briscoe, G. (2014). *Digital Innovation: The hackathon phenomenon.*

Brown, T. (2008). Design thinking. *Harvard Business Review, 86*(84–92), 141.

Chan, T., McMurray, J., Levy, A., Sveistrup, H., & Wallace, J. (2020). *Post-hackathon learning circles: Supporting lean startup development.*

Damanpour, F. (1991). Organizational innovation: A meta-analysis of effects of determinants and moderators. *The Academy of Management Journal, 34*(3), 555–590.

Decker, A., Eiselt, K., & Voll, K. (2015). *Understanding and improving the culture of hackathons: Think global hack local.* Paper presented at the IEEE Frontiers on Education Conference.

Desouza, K. C. (2011). *Intrapreneurship: Managing ideas within your organization.* University of Toronto Press.

Dysvik, A., & Kuvaas, B. (2011). Intrinsic motivation as a moderator on the relationship between perceived job autonomy and work performance. *European Journal of Work and Organizational Psychology, 20*, 367–387.

Furr, N., & Dyer, J. (2014). *The Innovator's method: Bringing the lean start-up into your organization.* Harvard Business Review Press.

Grant, A., Berry, J., Gino, F., Henifin, T., Myers, C., Brien, M., & Whelan, M. (2011). The necessity of others is the mother of invention: Intrinsic and prosocial motivations, perspective taking, and creativity. *Academy of Management Journal, 54*, 73–96.

Hammond, M., Neff, N., Farr, J., Schwall, A., & Zhao, X. (2011). Predictors of individual-level innovation at work: A meta-analysis. *Psychology of Aesthetics, Creativity, and the Arts, 5*, 90–105.

Harrison, S., Carlsen, A., & Škerlavaj, M. (2019). *Marvel's blockbuster machine*. Harvard Business Review.

Hlača Ferjančič et al. (2019). *Vodenje s posluhom 5/5: Med kreativnostjo in Excelom*. https://val202.rtvslo.si/2019/12/poslovno-gospodarske-teme-20/

Hlača Ferjančič et al. (2020). *Vodenje s posluhom: Vodenje notranjega podjetništva*. https://val202.rtvslo.si/2020/09/poslovno-gospodarske-teme-42/

Hærem, T., Pentland, B., & Miller, K. (2014). Task complexity: Extending a core concept. *The Academy of Management Review, 40*(3), 446–460.

Krapež Trošt, J., & Škerlavaj, M. (2016). Should our heart rule our head? Team innovation through intuition and rationality. In M. Škerlavaj, M. Černe, A. Dysvik, & A. Carlsen (Eds.), *Capitalizing on creativity at work: Fostering the implementation of creative ideas in organizations*. Edward Elgar.

Krapež Trošt, J., Škerlavaj, M., & Anzengruber, J. (2016). The ability–motivation–opportunity framework for team innovation: Efficacy beliefs, proactive personalities, supportive supervision and team innovation. *Economic and Business Review, 18*(1), 77–102.

Miron-Spektor, E., Erez, M., & Naveh, E. (2011). The effect of conformist and attentive-to-detail members on team innovation: Reconciling the innovation paradox. *The Academy of Management Journal, 54*(4), 740–760.

Nolte, A., Chounta, I. A., & Herbsleb, J. D. (2020). *What happens to all these hackathon projects? Identifying factors to promote hackathon project continuatio*. Paper presented at the Proceedings of the ACM on Human-Computer Interaction.

Ostenwalder, A., & Pigneur, Y. (2010). *Business model generation: A handbook for visionaries, game changers, and challengers*. Wiley.

Pink, D. H. (2011). *Drive*. Riverhead Books.

Prieto, L., Phipps, S., & Kungu, K. (2020). Facilitating a culture of intrapreneurship: An employee involvement approach. *Strategic HR Review, 19*, 93–95. https://doi.org/10.1108/SHR-04-2020-181

Rosenbusch, N., Brinckmann, J., & Bausch, A. (2011). Is innovation always beneficial? A meta-analysis of the relationship between innovation and performance in SMEs. *Journal of Business Venturing, 26*(4), 441–457.

Saks, A., Uggerslev, K., & Fassina, N. (2007). Socialization tactics and newcomer adjustment: A meta-analytic review and test of a model. *Journal of Vocational Behavior, 70*, 413–446.

Škerlavaj, M., Černe, M., Dysvik, A., & Carlsen, A. (2016). *Capitalizing on creativity at work: Fostering the implementation of creative ideas in organizations*. Edward Elgar.

Sluss, D. M., & Thompson, B. S. (2012). Socializing the newcomer: The mediating role of leader–member exchange. *Organizational Behavior and Human Decision Processes, 119*(1), 114–125.

Wong, S. I., Skerlavaj, M., & Černe, M. (2016). Build coalitions to fit: Autonomy expectations, competence mobilization, and job crafting. *Human Resource Management, 56*(5), 785–801.

Wood, R. E. (1986). Task complexity: Definition of the construct. *Organizational Behavior and Human Decision Processes, 37*(1), 60–82.

CHAPTER 9

Post-Heroic Leadership, Resilience, and Well-Being

Abstract Post-heroic leaders can nurture team and organization resilience by firstly being resilient themselves and helping individual members to overcome personal and professional struggles. The concept of resilience has to be understood from both individual and team level, due to their interdependence. Both types can be strengthened by focusing on people and by changing the perspective. Building resilience is especially important in the culture of always on, to mitigate the effects of panic work and excessive activation in times of social distancing, reduced socialization and increased uncertainty. The role of leaders is to humanize work to increase employee well-being.

Keywords Resilience · Well-being · Stress · Social distancing · Panic work · Uncertainty

Periods of increased stress often result in reduced subjective and even objective well-being (Helliwell et al., 2014; Van Hal, 2015) and the need for increased resilience of individuals, teams, and organizations. And even in the times of business as usual, researchers go as far as warning against the burnout epidemic and the rise of chronic stress (Moss, 2021). From a relatively obscure topic of research interest, resilience turned out to be one of the most mainstream areas of research and practice over last few

M. Škerlavaj, *Post-Heroic Leadership*,
https://doi.org/10.1007/978-3-030-90820-1_9

years. While the reasons are obvious, the role of post-heroic leadership is less so. Let us explore how post-heroic leaders can nurture resilience among their employees, teams, and in their organizations.

9.1 Resilience and Post-Heroic Leadership

Southwick et al. (2014) define resilience as:

> /…/ healthy functioning after a very unpleasant event; a conscious effort to move forward in a smart and positive way as a result of lessons learned through difficult times; the ability of the system to successfully adapt to disturbances that threaten its survival, functioning, and development.

First, resilient organizations and teams are formed by resilient individuals (Škerlavaj, 2020). Facebook Vice President Sheryl Sandberg and Wharton Professor Adam Grant (2017) wrote a touching personal story in the book Option B, which is about Sheryl being left alone with her two young children after her husband's tragic death. With Adam's help, she wrote a diary, a rather classic psychotherapeutic method that helped her find sources of resilience within herself, as well as in the support provided to her by her family and friends. The book not only describes the process of finding the resilience of the person concerned, but also presents the findings of research that help us understand and strengthen the resilience of individuals, teams, and organizations.

The role of post-heroic leadership in helping individual overcome their personal and professional struggles in building psychological resilience is quintessential. Tomaž Lanišek, former director of Knauf Insulation, took a sabbatical year to strengthen his resilience, which he spent at one of the most prestigious business schools, and now runs a smart city project in the Municipality of Kranj. Mr. Lanišek reflects upon his own learning and approaches towards building individual resilience:

> I had a privilege last year, I was able to take a sabbatical,l or a study leave, which after some 20 years of career really comes in handy, on the one hand to calm down, on the other hand to gain new insights at school. Build on them and then of course apply them here. Sometimes you need this reset to actively and one hundred percent dedicate yourself. /…/ It is precisely this resilience in leadership, in motivating people, where even artificial intelligence does not show any real effects, that is where the human future is very open and interesting. (Hlača Ferjančič et al., 2020)

Scholars have emphasized the need to understand resilience not only at the individual level but also at the team level (Alliger et al., 2015; King et al., 2016; Stoverink et al., 2018) and have begun to empirically explore the antecedents and outcomes of team resilience (Meneghel et al., 2016; Stephens et al., 2013). Since individual and team resilience are interdependent constructs and may influence each other, the literature encourages the adoption of a multilevel lens to study resilience (Hartmann et al., 2020).

Sluss and Powley (2020) argue that leaders in organizations can strengthen team resilience in two main ways. The first one is to focus on people. You need to know the resilience factors of your own team. These are, above all, a high level of self-confidence, disciplined work routines, and social and family support. Resilience can be strengthened with a relatively simple measure such as time blocking. The director of AMZS, the largest provider of roadside assistance in Slovenia, and the winner of the Young Manager Award 2019, Lucija Sajevec, confided during the School of Economics and Business webinar series SEB LU Contributes that they have also used the time blocking technique (Aleksić et al., 2020). Shortly after the epidemic was declared, they established a morning-hours routine as a time for meetings, blocking lunch time, and then an afternoon-hours routine as a time to follow up on appointments and implement the agreed actions. All of this provides at least some degree of predictability in times when everything else is unknown.

In addition to a sincere concern for high-quality relationships and understanding, special care is needed for the profile of people who are by nature very helpful and conscientious. This is a combination of personality traits that is typically a characteristic of successful people and is beneficial to the organizations in which they operate. Paradoxically, in challenging times of over-activation, this same combination of helpfulness and diligence poses a significantly increased risk of burnout. To avoid panic work and to increase predictability, Sluss and Powley (2020) suggests focusing on long-term, strategic initiatives for people with such a personality profile.

The second way to strengthen team resilience is to change perspective. Meta-analytical research (Vanhove et al., 2016) shows that quality and personalized coaching is invaluable in strengthening resilience. U.S. marines who have been subjected to numerous psycho-physical trials have shown 20% greater resilience and endurance using the coaching method. Fear and anxiety dampen the ability to look to the future and find much needed creative solutions. On the other hand, asking the right kind of questions helps. Interestingly, these are not the ones that show us the world through rose-coloured glasses, as superficial believers in positive psychology might imagine.

Interviews among World War II camp survivors, for example, showed that the greatest optimists died first. The reason was the broken heart syndrome. The survivors were those who knew how to face reality immediately (Coutu, 2002), and realized that they were not alone and that they could rely on and cooperate with others in overcoming the accumulated problems. The last set of measures to strengthen team resilience is learning. Leaders of resistant teams find opportunities to learn because of the crisis, not in spite of it. Identifying the hidden champions and special talents that show up in changed circumstances is the key. All these measures help build resilient individuals, teams, and organizations, who do not only face but also shape the new normal.

Let us have a look at an example from the culinary world. While it is not unusual for top chefs to possess the uncertainty mindset (Tan, 2020), the world's best female chef Ana Roš and her two Michelin star restaurant Hiša Franko showed some remarkable resilience during lockdown (Sajovic, 2020 in Škerlavaj, 2020). In March 2020, her international team just gathered after the winter break to face COVID-19 with devastating consequences for the entire hospitality industry. Instead of sending people off, most of the team decided to stay in the "green jail", as Ana Roš liked to put it.

Not being used to sitting idle, Ana engaged her team in ideation workshops that resulted in a series of products and even business model innovations. Wild grass kombucha, fermented flowers of wild magnolia, garum from local lamb, and forest-taste popcorn all led to developing an offering of high-end mountain "fast food" that is being packaged and sent across Europe to foodies unable to travel in person. To deal with the excess of wine (Hiša Franko works with natural wine producers from across Slovenia), the sommelier team also set up an online wine shop. Furthermore, Ana Roš started partnering with Tuš, one of major Slovenian retailer brand, and created a line of gourmet food under her personal brand, widely accessible via the online and offline stores.

Partnering with the local dairy farm Mlekarna Planika, which was left with a surplus of fresh milk, Hiša Franko developed an offering of mountain ice creams with forest and mountain flavours, such as bee pollen or sour milk with candied pine nuts. True enough, these are not activities to replace but rather complement the core business and predominantly serve as a tool to build a resilient organization (Škerlavaj, 2020).

Mrs. Anka Lipušček Miklavič, director of dairy company Mlekarna Planika that Ana Roš was collaborating with, is locally known as a director who milks cows at five in the morning, and then goes and runs a serious business. The world got to know her through the story of Ana Roš and her famous Chef's Table documentary on Netflix (2016). Mrs. Lipušček Miklavič reflects upon the collaboration as a tool for resilience:

> I think it's the fact that the Soča Valley where we live and work is so cramped, it has placed us so close to each other that we just can't escape and so we have to cooperate. We must work together if we want to survive. Be it a product, an action, after all you mentioned Ana Roš, her story. Today the stories sell. And is there anything more beautiful than our story, offered to us by the beautiful nature in the Soča Valley. This story is strong enough to connect the inhabitants of the valley. (Hlača Ferjančič et al., 2020)

Mr. Lipušček Miklavič recalls the times of hardship when the cooperative established the dairy farm:

> In the beginning, the agricultural cooperative founded this dairy. The first director was Mr. Maver, and a team was formed. The first battle line consists of department heads: the head of sales, the head of production, the head of technologies, the head buyer, who takes care of milk purchases. And then we have other members of the team. (Hlača Ferjančič et al., 2020)

She also recalls the most recent challenge of COVID-19 crisis when the organizational resilience has been again put to the challenge:

> We worked all the time, except for those employed in the store where the working schedule was shortened, and they adjusted to all the prescribed schedules. In the production, we worked normally all the time, perhaps even harder because we lost quite a bit of market for fresh produce overnight. We recorded a large drop in sales of fresh milk, which has a short shelf life, because shopping habits have changed. People were going to the store less often, and we had to react to that change. (Hlača Ferjančič et al., 2020)
>
> So, we made cheese from everything. In all my history in the company we have never been making cheese in two shifts, but this year we have

> done that. We made quite a nice amount of cheese, because that is the only product where the milk can wait longer. In addition, we dedicated a part of the milk to long life milk, UHT milk, and in this way solved the purchase of milk in the Soča Valley region, so there wasn't a day when milk would not be picked up from the local farms. We consider this to be a great success. If I connect it with experience or leadership – here I can really say that it is good to have some experience, I can't imagine what it would be like if this happened right at the beginning of my career in the dairy. Experience and perhaps some greater prudence can also help in a situation like this. (Hlača Ferjančič et al., 2020)

While she praises the team, she also recognizes the role post-heroic leaders have in collective resilience. Her metaphor is picturesque:

> I also say it to the team: I am aware of my function, to be hitched to the cart in the front. But if all those in the back or beside the cart don't push in the same direction, that power from before will be lost and the cart will no longer move in the right direction. And it is important that we work as equals and stick together. We are all co-creating this story and we all need to be aware that we work for the same goal; the milk producers, cheesemakers, shop assistants, workers in the cafeteria and our employees on the ecological estate in Bovec. Each is an extremely important link in the chain we form together. I don't want to assign any credit, as I think that if everyone plays their part in this story, then we can create one common good story. If only one comes loose, then this chain, this community or this cooperation is broken. (Hlača Ferjančič et al., 2020)

9.2 Post-Heroic Leadership and Well-Being in the Age of Disruption

Remember the times before the COVID-19 pandemic? In Scandinavia, they were experimenting with a six-hour workday (Alderman, 2016; Anttila et al., 2005). The aim was to achieve that technological progress, in addition to increased productivity at work, would also be reflected in a higher quality of life. Germans and French were disconnecting work servers at night to cut through the disease of the modern world, when it is necessary to be always, everywhere, and immediately available. There has been talk of digital detoxification (Syvertsen, 2020) and need to fight always-on cultures at work (McDowall & Kinman, 2017). But then the virus hit and before in many places the timid digital transformation switched to steroids, working from home became a new reality.

Aleksić and Černe (2020) reported, that as many as 60% of participants in their pilot study perceive the pressures of the so-called always on culture in their organizations. Many of us who deal with services have moved to garages, we have occupied children's rooms, dining tables and what was left of suitable flat surfaces, connected to the Internet and worked like crazy. The desire for a six-hour workday has become a reality of twelve hours plus, and for seven days a week.

Petriglieri (in Kale, 2020) coined the word zoombies as half-living, half-dead creatures, spending endless hours each in front of their own screen, trying to communicate and do business with the world through their zoom profile and other similar virtual communication tools.

The first response to the new situation was, as expected, excessive activation. Panic work, which is nothing but a manic-defensive response. In the initial stages of the epidemic, several companies also reported the opening of scissors between high levels of job satisfaction and low levels of life satisfaction in general. Which is by no means a sustainable situation, as such discrepancies are also associated with poorer mental health (especially anxiety, stress, and burnout), resulting from social distancing and significantly reduced socialization.

Humans are social animals, and neuroscientist Mathew Lieberman (2013) has shown, that the density of our brain connections correlates with the density and quality of our social connections with fellow humans around us. Therefore, we are wired to connect. Somewhat in the shadow of daily media reports on the health status of the population and regular speculation about economic intervention measures, interest in the psychological or human dimension of the problem has also grown.

Zacher and Rudolph (2020) monitored nearly a thousand German individuals and their subjective perception of well-being through the early stages of the COVID-19 pandemic in the period between December 2019 and May 2020. If there were no changes between December 2019 and March 2019, the differences between March and May 2020 are obvious. On average, life satisfaction deteriorated, with positive emotion levels lower and negative emotion levels higher among German survey participants. The pandemic continues, as does the research.

It is already clear that the German study is mostly about the effects of reduced socialization and increased uncertainty. Therefore, it is interesting that neuroscientific research showed that highly anxious people have more intense neurological reactions to uncertainty than to negative feedback. So, when we are anxious, we need more certainty. The period of uncertainty will continue for quite some time.

These finding apply to physical work settings as well. One of the central themes for post-heroic leadership action seems to be the well-being of employees. Mrs. Lipuščček Miklavič, director of the dairy company Mlekarna Planika reflects about the need for leaders to see their employees and partners in whole:

> Everyone in the company knows each other. If you go to a person, because you know them, you know their family, and you ask them how they are doing, how are their parents, if you have such an attitude, a human attitude towards an employee, it seems that it does a lot for the atmosphere itself, in motivating employees. We also organize various trainings, various gatherings, to somehow connect people with each other. We had a practice that every year we went to see some other production, outside of dairy production.
>
> We visited all the wine cellars of the Coastal region of Slovenia, among other things, and this also contributes to motivation, to actually see how it is elsewhere; how others work, that they also have to fight as we have to fight. They know that my job is to say what has to be done if we want to succeed. The milk that comes to the dairy needs to be processed, and no matter how easy it is, or how hard it is, you need to make something out of it, be it cheese or cottage cheese or yogurt. The workers know that it is necessary, but on the other hand, I think that if you approach them in a more personal way, then they also know how to appreciate it. (Hlača Ferjančič et al., 2020)

At the same time, post-heroic leaders need to be aware of the need to replenish their own well-being by utilizing the uncertainty mindset. Mrs. Lipuščček Miklavič explains her own approach as well as idea of problem reduction:

> We are all human beings, and we all need various boosters so that we can start the day, tackle the next problem, and solve it in such a way that it affects you a little less than it would otherwise. I think I should maybe escape into the mountains a bit more, if time would allow, because then I could probably do even more for myself and others. One of the things I learned during these years is that the problems of today need to be solved today. Those that may or may not come tomorrow, we will solve

> tomorrow, we will not tackle them today, because there are enough others to solve today. (Hlača Ferjančič et al., 2020)

Mr. Lanišek provides some additional thoughts on how to strengthen resilience as a leader to be able to support employee, team, and organizational resilience further down the line:

> Personally, I am quite an athlete and I do a lot of sports. The key is when you work, you work; when you have your private life, you use it as actively as possible, of course with your family. If you know how to switch from this business to private and vice versa, it is worth the most. It is not always easy, but if you succeed, it is important. (Hlača Ferjančič et al., 2020)

Mrs. Lipušček Miklavič reiterates the importance of post-heroic leadership as a shared and servant process that contributes to the well-being of everyone involved, including the leaders:

> I would just say: be persistent, never give up, pick yourself up when you fall and have co-workers by your side, who will give you a hand when you're on the ground. /.../ My knees have been very bruised, I still have some scratches from the beginning of my career, but they have already faded. The falls were quite harsh, but I gained experience from them as well. If I say from my own experience: yes, you can do it, if there is a vision, and if you see the goal in front of you. But the journey matters more than your goal. (Hlača Ferjančič et al., 2020)

In other words, the role of post-heroic leaders in increasing well-being of employees is to humanize work. It is an adage as old as life, yet we still need to be reminded of it. Hundred-year-old Hawthorne study actually found that while researchers expected improved physical working conditions will lead to improved productivity (Snow, 1927), it was the socio-social element that was crucial (Mayo, 1933; Roethlisberger & Dickinson, 1939). These studies have been revisited and replicated in more recent times (Zhong & House, 2012). That is, you see someone, you ask them how they are, how their family is; so that they feel as a part of one collective. In organizational lives, we should be aware that we are all so close and so interdependent that we could be more cooperative, more sensible with each other.

References

Alderman, L. (2016). In Sweden, an experiment turns shorter workdays into bigger gains. *The New York Times*.

Aleksić, D., & Černe, M. (2020, junij/julij). Ko prožno delo postane nuja. *HR&M revija*. https://www.hrm-revija.si/koprozno- delo-postane-nuja

Aleksić, D., Černe, M., & Sajevec, L. (2020). *Kako dolgo lahko zaposleni "zmrzujemo" na daljavo?: CPOEF "E-talk."* University of Ljubljana.

Alliger, G. M., Cerasoli, C. P., Tannenbaum, S. I., & Vessey, W. B. (2015). Team resilience: How teams flourish under pressure. *Organizational Dynamics, 44*(3), 176–184.

Anttila, T., Nätti, J., & Väisänen, M. (2005). The experiments of reduced working hours in Finland. *Community, Work & Family, 8*(2), 187–209.

Coutu, D. L. (2002). How resilience works. *Harvard Business Review, 80*(5), 46–56.

Grant, A., & Sandberg, S. (2017). Option B: Facing adversity, building resilience, and finding joy. *The New York Times*, 620.

Hartmann, S., Weiss, M., Newman, A., & Hoegl, M. (2020). Resilience in the workplace: A multilevel review and synthesis. *Applied Psychology, 69*(3), 913–959.

Helliwell, J., Huang, H., & Wang, S. (2014). Social Capital and Well-Being in Times of Crisis. *Journal of Happiness Studies, 15*. https://doi.org/10.1007/s10902-013-9441-z

Hlača Ferjančič et al. (2020). *Vodenje s posluhom: Krepitev odpornosti vodij*. https://val202.rtvslo.si/2020/09/poslovno-gospodarske-teme-41/

Kale, S. (2020). *Working from home? Video conference call tips for the self-isolating*.

King, D. D., Newman, A., & Luthans, F. (2016). Not if, but when we need resilience in the workplace. *Journal of Organizational Behavior, 37*(5), 782–786.

Lieberman, M. D. (2013). *Social: Why our brains are wired to connect*. Crown.

Mayo, E. (1933). *The human problems of an industrial civilization*. Macmillan.

McDowall, A., & Kinman, G. (2017). The new nowhere land? A research and practice agenda for the "always on culture". *Journal of Organizational Effectiveness: People and Performance, 4*(3), 256–266.

Meneghel, I., Borgogni, L., Miraglia, M., Salanova, M., & Martínez, I. M. (2016). From social context and resilience to performance through job satisfaction: A multilevel study over time. *Human Relations, 69*(11), 2047–2067.

Moss, J. (2021). *The burnout epidemic: The rise of chronic stress and how we can fix it*. Harvard Business Review Press.

Netflix. (2016). *Chef's Table* (A. Fuller, Dir.). Ana Roš.

Petriglieri, G. (2020). We are all Zoombies now, but it has to stop. *Financial Times*.

Roethlisberger, F. J., & Dickinson, W. J. (1939). *Management and the worker.* Harvard University Press.

Škerlavaj, M. (2020). New normal, new leaders? Time for resilience and post-heroic leadership. In P. Domadenik, M. Koman, & T. Redek (Eds.), *The virus aftermath: a socio-economic twist?* (1st ed., pp. 347–362). Časnik Finance.

Sluss, D., & Powley, E. (2020). Build your team's resilience—From home. *Harvard Business Review*, April 14, 2021. https://hbr.org/2020/04/build-your-teams-resilience-from-home

Snow, C. E. (1927). *Research on industrial illumination: A discussion of the relation of illumination intensity to productive efficiency* (Vol. 8, pp. 272–282). Tech Engineering News.

Southwick, S. M., Bonanno, G. A., Masten, A. S., Panter-Brick, C., & Yehuda, R. (2014). Resilience definitions, theory, and challenges: Interdisciplinary perspectives. *European Journal of Psychotraumatology, 5*(1), 25338.

Stephens, J. P., Heaphy, E. D., Carmeli, A., Spreitzer, G. M., & Dutton, J. E. (2013). Relationship quality and virtuousness: Emotional carrying capacity as a source of individual and team resilience. *The Journal of Applied Behavioral Science, 49*(1), 13–41.

Stoverink, A. C., Chiaburu, D. S., Li, N., & Zheng, X. (2018). Supporting team citizenship: The influence of team social resources on team-level affiliation-oriented and challenge-oriented behaviour. *Human Resource Management Journal, 28*(2), 201–215.

Syvertsen, T. (2020). *Digital detox: The politics of disconnecting.*

Tan, V. (2020). *The uncertainty mindset: Innovation insights from the frontiers of food.* Columbia University Press.

Van Hal, G. (2015). The true cost of the economic crisis on psychological well-being: A review. *Psychology Research and Behavior Management, 8*, 17.

Vanhove, A. J., Herian, M. N., Perez, A. L. U., Harms, P. D., & Lester, P. B. (2016). Can resilience be developed at work? A meta-analytic review of resilience-building programme effectiveness. *Journal of Occupational and Organizational Psychology, 89*(2), 278–307.

Zacher, H., & Rudolph, C. (2020). Individual differences and changes in subjective wellbeing during the early stages of the COVID-19 pandemic. *American Psychologist, 76*(1), 50–62.

Zhong, C.-B., & House, J. (2012). Hawthorne revisited: Organizational implications of the physical work environment. *Research in Organizational Behavior, 32*, 3–22.

CHAPTER 10

Post-Heroic Leadership: Epilogue and Agenda for Future Research and Action

Abstract To tackle the complex challenges of today we need leaders who know how to focus on the task and put themselves in the supporting role. Post-heroic leadership has the potential to be the type of leadership best suited for this task. Qualitative research evidence based on interviews with post-heroic leaders explored various topics related to the nature of work and presented a conceptual model of post-heroic leadership. Post-heroic leadership represents a way of moving away from micromanagement and towards strengthening healthy relationships and fostering innovation. It also shows how to face wicked problems without dehumanizing work.

Keywords Interview data · Post-heroic leaders · Newer-genre leadership theory · Conceptual model · Follower

When we as a society and as organizations tackle the largest issues, there is no room for the ego. Instead, we need leaders who know how to actively involve and connect. Responsible people who know how to put the task and the team of experts in the foreground, and themselves in the background (Galunic, 2020; Škerlavaj, 2020). With the surge of newer-genre forms of leadership (Hannah et al., 2014), post-heroic leadership has the potential to address the mounting challenges of the present and future.

M. Škerlavaj, *Post-Heroic Leadership*,
https://doi.org/10.1007/978-3-030-90820-1_10

This book is a humble attempt to contribute to the growing field of newer-genre leadership theories. It adds to the previous body of literature by developing a conceptual model of the context, process, and outcomes of post-heroic leadership. While publications on the integral elements of shared and servant leadership are plentiful, the publications on post-heroic leadership have been less prevalent up to date. They are needed to successfully manage complex situations in front and ahead of us.

10.1 Conceptual Model of Post-Heroic Leadership

Post-heroic leadership is a second-order construct with three distinctive characteristics: sharedness, interdependence, and servantship (Fletcher, 2004). Specifically, shared leadership as a first-order construct of post-heroic leadership means sharing the purpose among organizational members and the leader, providing social support, and facilitating voice behaviours. Dimensions of servant leadership include empowerment, humility, authenticity, interpersonal acceptance, providing direction, and stewardship. The qualitative research evidence based on interviews with post-heroic leaders clearly demonstrates presence, depth, and scale of those leadership styles.

Context in which post-heroic leadership enters the big stage is the context of significant uncertainty. COVID-19 crisis lifted the idea of VUCA world to the new level, and numerous organizations around the globe need to find better and smarter ways of addressing their business environments. Those challenges are far from isolated and will not seize to exist in the future. Post-heroic leadership has the potential to address the wicked challenges of the future and therefore deserves our research as well as practical attention.

Special attention was given to the changing nature of work and rise of hybridity. Leaders around the world are adapting their leadership approaches to situations where the organization is suddenly no longer a group of more or less collocated individuals coordinating their activities to achieve common goals. At least not all the time. Instead, the challenge for most leaders is to keep together people who do at least a significant part of their work remotely.

This book joins the call for further humanization of work (Hamel & Zanini, 2020) and stepping away from algorithmic management.

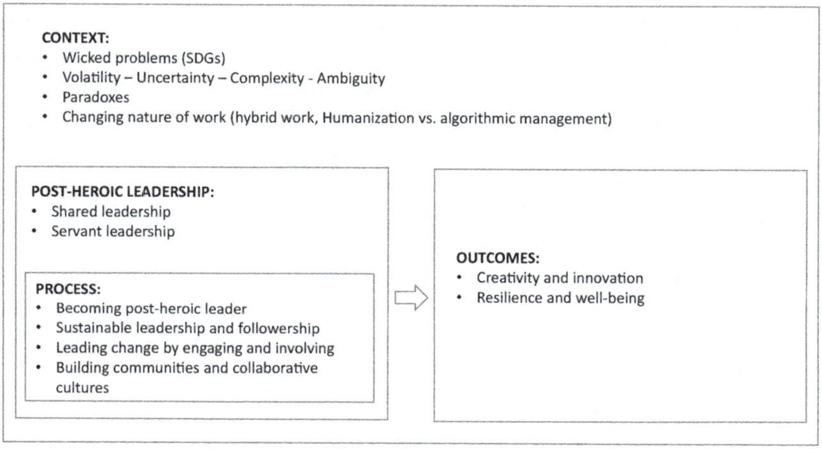

Fig. 10.1 Conceptual model of post-heroic leadership

Figure 10.1 depicts the conceptual model of post-heroic leadership, its context, process, as well as selected salient outcomes.

The process of post-heroic leadership as described includes the act of becoming a leader, from the often-experienced transition from top expert to rather inexperienced, even amateur leader. We explore ideas of selection and development of post-heroic leaders. As leadership is always a relational process and by definition does not exist without followers, the book also explores how to change followers' implicit leadership theories to expect less heroism and more behaviours associated with post-heroic leadership.

As such, the central idea of post-heroic leadership is also related to sustainability. We argue that post-heroic leadership is the missing piece of the sustainability puzzle that can make organizational life sustainable for both followers and leaders. The next important question the book addresses is the way post-heroic leaders approach change by engaging and involving the followers. Through the shared and servant leadership style, post-heroic leaders develop employee psychological ownership of change content and process and improve cognitive and affective reactions needed for success of change initiatives. Own research also provides evidence and exemplifies how post-heroic leaders build communities and collaborative cultures.

While there are numerous implications of post-heroic leadership, the book focuses on several sets of consequences. First, we examine the role of post-heroic leadership in creativity and innovation. The first central argument is that post-heroic leaders need to utilize innovative working methods that build upon human centeredness, experimentation, and iterativity. Second, post-heroic leaders need to and did in fact engage in building organizational cultures that are supportive of innovation. Third, from a niche topic, resilience became a mainstream idea. Post-heroic leadership has a proven track record in stimulating resilient individuals, teams, and organizations. Fourth, in the era of major disruptions, post-heroic leadership needs to dedicate its attention to subjective and objective well-being.

10.2 Agenda for Future Research

The previously depicted and described conceptual model of the process, content, and outcomes of the post-heroic leadership contributes to a research topic that has been around for thirty years. Still, it is in its' nascent phase. True enough, knowledge about its building blocks of servant (Hoch et al., 2016; Langhof & Güldenberg, 2019) and shared (D'Innocenzo et al., 2016; Bolden et al., 2015; Martin et al., 2018; Scott-Young et al., 2019; Sweeney et al., 2019) leadership has progressed significantly. We still need integrative studies that will move the field forward. As our qualitative data indicates, shared and servant elements of post-heroic leadership are often intertwined to address relevant challenges of present and future.

Future researchers are invited to further develop and test the proposed model using quantitative studies to increase the generalizability of our findings. While this study did its best to develop a practice-based, process model of post-heroic leadership, I do not claim it is an exhaustive list of antecedents, nor consequences related to post-heroic leadership. Future studies should revolve around extending and deepening the nomological network of post-heroic leadership. Future studies should also aim to overcome the mismatch between theoretical and analytical strategies used (Klein & Kozlowski, 2012; Kozlowski & Klein, 2012). Previously used studies often claim to, e.g., use relational type of theory while applying single level analytical research approach.

10.3 Agenda for Future Action

Post-heroic leadership, like its complementary newer-genre leadership styles, contributes to wake of humanocracy (Hamel & Zanini, 2020; Schein & Schein, 2018). For a long time now, there has been an increase in the so-called algorithmic management (Kellogg et al., 2019; Wood et al., 2018), which is projected in various forms and manifestations. I argued extensively in the third chapter, that this kind of approach towards leading people is a bigger part of the problem than the solution and suggest post-heroic leadership practices as those that can help modern leaders in creating better solution to current and future wicked problems. We learnt that post-heroic leadership contributes to mastering change processes by engaging and involving and develops creative, innovative solutions while maintaining physical and psychological well-being of employees and leaders.

I also discussed accelerated digital transformation and redefining future of work, where the main challenge is how to do well by doing good. Meaning, benefiting organizations by adoption of new technologies and approaches to work without dehumanizing it.

The times are decisive, and the actions taken during these turbulences will remain rooted in organizational systems and cultures long after the storms are over. It is time for action and change agency towards a smarter, more humane, and more sustainable life and work. It is also time to build helpful and collaborative cultures. Post-heroic leaders can contribute. So can each one of us. I sincerely hope that this book was a small, yet important building stone in doing so.

References

Bolden, R., Jones, S., Davis, H., & Gentle, P. (2015). *Developing and sustaining shared leadership in higher education*. http://hdl.handle.net/11343/55439

D'Innocenzo, L., Mathieu, J. E., & Kukenberger, M. R. (2016). A meta-analysis of different forms of shared leadership–team performance relations. *Journal of Management, 42*(7), 1964–1991.

Fletcher, J. K. (2004). The paradox of postheroic leadership: An essay on gender, power, and transformational change. *The Leadership Quarterly, 15*(5), 647–661.

Galunic, C. (2020). *Backstage leadership: The invisible work of highly effective leaders*. Springer Nature.

Hamel, G., & Zanini, M. (2020). *Humanocracy: Creating organizations as amazing as the people inside them*. Harvard Business Press.
Hannah, S. T., Sumanth, J. J., Lester, P., & Cavarretta, F. (2014). Debunking the false dichotomy of leadership idealism and pragmatism: Critical evaluation and support of newer genre leadership theories. *Journal of Organizational Behavior, 35*(5), 598–621.
Hoch, J. E., Bommer, W. H., Dulebohn, J. H., & Wu, D. (2016). Do ethical, authentic, and servant leadership explain variance above and beyond transformational leadership? A Meta-Analysis. *Journal of Management, 44*(2), 501–529.
Kellogg, K. C., Valentine, M. A., & Christin, A. (2019). Algorithms at work: The new contested terrain of control. *Academy of Management Annals, 14*(1), 366–410.
Klein, K., & Kozlowski, S. (2012). *Multilevel theory, research, and methods in organizations: Foundations, extensions, and new directions*. Jossey-Bass.
Kozlowski, S., & Klein, K. (2012). A multilevel approach to theory and research in organizations: Contextual, temporal, and emergent processes. In *Multilevel theory, research, and methods in organizations: Foundations, extensions, and new directions*. Jossey-Bass.
Langhof, J. G., & Güldenberg, S. (2019). Servant leadership: A systematic literature review—Toward a model of antecedents and outcomes. *German Journal of Human Resource Management, 34*(1), 32–68.
Martin, J., Cormican, K., Sampaio, S. C. B., & Wu, Q. (2018). Shared leadership and team performance: An analysis of moderating factors. *Procedia Computer Science, 138*, 671–679.
Schein, E. H., & Schein, P. A. (2018). *Humble Leadership*. Berrett-Koehler Publishers.
Scott-Young, C. M., Georgy, M., & Grisinger, A. (2019). Shared leadership in project teams: An integrative multi-level conceptual model and research agenda. *International Journal of Project Management, 37*(4), 565–581.
Škerlavaj, M. (2020). New normal, new leaders? Time for resilience and post-heroic leadership. In P. Domadenik, M. Koman, & T. Redek (Eds.), *The virus aftermath: A socio-economic twist?* (1st ed., pp. 347–362). Časnik Finance.
Sweeney, A., Clarke, N., & Higgs, M. (2019). Shared leadership in commercial organizations: A systematic review of definitions, theoretical frameworks and organizational outcomes. *International Journal of Management Reviews, 21*(1), 115–136.
Wood, A., Graham, M., Lehdonvirta, V., & Hjorth, I. (2018). *Good gig, bad big: Autonomy and algorithmic control in the global gig economy* (p. 33). Employment and Society.

Index

A

Abductive research design, 16
Algorithmic management, 106, 107, 186, 189
Always-on culture, 105, 128, 178, 179
Authenticity, 11, 186
Autonomy, 104, 106, 116, 125, 135, 161, 162

B

Burnout, 104, 128, 173, 175, 179

C

Change leadership, 13, 127, 136, 137, 187
Coaching, 11, 175
Collaboration, 7, 105, 137, 177
Community, 5, 14, 15, 126, 146–148, 150, 151, 178
Competence, 13, 15, 115, 118, 163
Complex problems, 7
Conceptual model, 12, 186–188
Context, 7, 10, 13, 104, 105, 114, 115, 126, 138, 146, 149, 150, 161, 186, 187
Continuous innovation, 162–164, 166
COVID-19, 3, 4, 6, 13, 104, 107, 176–179, 186
Creativity, 108, 157–159, 161–165, 188
Culture, 108, 117, 126, 137, 141, 158, 163–168, 187, 189

D

Development, 11, 104, 128, 136, 137, 139, 140, 147, 150, 159, 160, 162, 166, 167, 174
Digital transformation, 7, 140, 141, 179, 189
Domain-specific knowledge, 114

E

Ego-free leadership, 3
Employee well-being, 124
Empowerment, 11, 116, 186

M. Škerlavaj, *Post-Heroic Leadership*,
https://doi.org/10.1007/978-3-030-90820-1

Engaging, 4, 106, 118, 135–138, 176, 187–189
Expert, 4, 6, 113, 114, 116–118, 141, 159, 185, 187
Expert leadership, 113

F
Feedback, 139, 150–152, 167, 168, 180
Flexible work, 105
Follower, 10–12, 16, 118, 124, 136, 187
Follower implicit leadership theory, 118
Future of work, 104, 167, 189

G
Golem effect, 107

H
Hackathon, 139, 167, 168
History of management, 106
HRM practices, 124, 126
Humanizing work, 106, 108, 181, 186
Human resources, 115, 124, 126, 165
Humility, 11, 118, 186
Hybrid work, 103, 105, 106, 108, 128

I
Innovation, 6, 7, 14, 108, 157–159, 161–164, 166–168, 176, 188
Innovation paradox, 158, 161, 162
Innovation techniques, 159
Interpersonal acceptance, 12, 117, 186
Interview data, 117, 163
Intrapreneurship, 166, 167
Involving, 4, 104, 117, 135–140, 148, 150, 158, 161, 167, 181, 185, 187, 189

L
Leader, 5, 10–14, 16, 113, 114, 116, 118–120, 127–129, 136, 138, 139, 145, 149, 152, 158, 165, 181, 186, 187
Leadership, 3–5, 9–11, 13, 15–16, 104, 105, 114–119, 124, 129, 137, 147, 151, 152, 158, 164, 174, 178, 185–188
Leadership competencies, 115, 118
Leadership development, 116, 124, 152, 162, 187
Leading change, 133, 134

M
Mental health, 5, 179
Micromanagement, 107
Motivation, 11, 115, 119, 127, 128, 136, 162, 180

N
Newer-genre leadership theory, 15, 186, 189

O
Organizational change, 133
Organizational culture, 7, 162, 188, 189
Outcome, 4, 175, 186–188
Overwork, 105, 160

P
Panic work, 175, 179
Paradox, 5, 6, 13, 15, 175

Positional leaders, 10
Process, 5, 10, 106, 115, 118, 134–136, 139, 147, 149, 152, 158, 159, 161, 163, 165, 167, 174, 180, 181, 186–189
Prosociality, 136, 162
Providing direction, 12, 117, 186
Psychological ownership, 136, 138, 187
Psychological safety, 106, 128, 149, 151, 168
Pygmalion effect, 108

R
Radical candour, 150
Relationship, 10, 108, 116, 124, 146, 149–152, 165, 175
Resilience, 108, 173–178, 188
Responsibility, 6, 10–12, 125, 140, 148

S
Scientific management, 106
Self-confidence, 13, 15, 175
Sense of belonging, 146
Servant leadership, 5, 9, 11, 12, 15, 16, 116, 117, 149, 186, 187
Shared leadership, 10, 16, 118, 129, 145, 186
Social distancing, 104, 179
Society, 5, 146, 185
Stakeholderism, 126
Start-up, 165–167
Stewardship, 12, 118, 186
Strengthening resilience, 127, 128, 174–176, 181
Stress, 105, 173, 179
Sustainability at work, 124
Sustainable development goals, 6, 13, 123
Sustainable leadership, 14, 124, 126, 128, 129

T
Taylorism, 106, 107

U
Uncertainty, 6, 13, 134, 152, 162, 176, 179, 180, 186

V
VUCA world, 4, 134, 186

W
Well-being, 12, 107, 124, 127, 128, 173, 178–181, 188
Wicked problems, 4, 6, 7, 189
Work from anywhere, 104, 105, 128, 164
Work from home, 104

The manufacturer's authorised representative in the EU is Springer Nature Customer Service Centre GmbH, Europaplatz 3, 69115 Heidelberg, Germany. If you have any concerns regarding our products, please contact ProductSafety@springernature.com

Printed and bound by CPI Group (UK) Ltd, Croydon, CR0 4YY
30/09/2026
02225502-0001